POLITICAL BLUES

POLITICAL BLUES

PETER GARRETT

HODDER AND STOUGHTON
SYDNEY AUCKLAND

ACKNOWLEDGEMENTS

The publisher and author acknowledge the assistance of staff and students at the School of Design, Randwick College of TAFE. All illustrations for this book are the work of first year students —

Cover design: Jacky Smith
Title page and preliminary pages design: Christopher Magus
Blackfella-Whitefella: Amos Wang
Advertising: Rainer Hug
Shall we dance: Di Roper
The Budget: Amos Wong
The Australia Card: Gemma Dickson
Kakadu: Mandy Carruth
Reykjavik Summit: Rodney Denson
Visits by nuclear-armed ships: Julie Geraghty
Hawke v. Lange: Di Roper
Constitutional Commission: Sharon Holloway
Assistance to the Arts: Petrea Doyle
The beat goes on: Christopher Magus
Anzus: David Spencer
Bicentenary: Jacky Smith
The New Right: Gaylyn Smith
Land Rights: Amos Wong
Queensland: Rodney Denson
In Vitro Fertilisation: Jane Weatherley
Sponsorship: Sophie Tourrier
Pine Gap: Stephanie Green
Back Cover Photograph: Adrienne Overall

First published in 1987
by Hodder and Stoughton (Australia) Pty Limited
2 Apollo Place, Lane Cove, NSW 2066
© text Peter Garrett
©illustrations copyright individual artists
National Library of Australia Cataloguing-in-Publication entry
Garrett, Peter, 1953–
  Political blues.
  Bibliography.
  Includes index.
  ISBN 0 340 42505 9
  1. Political science – Australia. 2. Australia – Politics and government – 1976 – . 3. Australia – Social conditions – 1976 – . I. Title.
320.994
Typeset by GT Setters, Kenthurst, NSW
Printed by Owen King Printers, Mulgrave, Victoria

CONTENTS

INTRODUCTION

In 1986 I was asked by a capital city newspaper to write a series of weekly columns for young readers on topical issues. And so the collection that is *Political Blues* was begun.

Unfortunately politics is a dirty word in Australia. I know that many people, particularly young Australians, are dismayed by the current political scene and can find no place in it for themselves.

I love my sunburnt country and yet it is a place uncertain of its future, not trusting its institutions, and reliant on an out-dated view of what is happening. The powerful groups in the community, in particular government and the large corporations, carry a great responsibility but as Bob Brown has said ". . . [their] access to money, information and the ears of power . . . drains the decency from democracy". The result, a kind of conservatism which is an impediment to social change and breeds prejudice. It is not good for Australia, for the land or the people.

I hope this book goes some way towards making us consider our future in a different light. I am confident that we can be active rather than passive and in that way participate in shaping our destiny, but to do this requires a major shift in values. Surely the only thing holding us back now is not believing we have the ability to take big steps. I hope this book helps us believe.

Peter Garrett, August 1987.

BLACKFELLA —
WHITEFELLA

One of the great problems facing Australia's European rulers since the arrival of the First Fleet has been the question of how to deal with the country's original inhabitants. Unfortunately, the solutions developed have had little basis in understanding and have been largely founded on ignorance. It is to be hoped that, as we approach the Bicentenary, Australians can at last acknowledge the depth and strength of Aboriginal culture so that our culture and theirs can co-exist far more peacefully and productively in the future than they have in the past.

Blackfella, whitefella
It doesn't matter, what your colour
As long as you're a true fella
As long as you're a real fella
We need more brothers if we're to make it
We need more sisters if we're to save it
Are you the one who's gonna stand up
*   and be counted?*

Warumpi Band

We were criminals. We were drunkards, thieves and adulterers. We'd been stuck in gaol for years and it was getting so crowded they decided to ship us half way around the world to live in somebody else's place. We got seasick a lot and when we arrived there was nothing but bush as far as the eye could see. There were some people with black skin living there. The soldiers who were with us shot as many as they could. These people didn't speak English. We thought they'd come from Africa.

We thought that we were superior to these Australian Aborigines (which is what they were eventually called) because we had more clothes on than they did, even if we still had leg irons on and chains around our ankles plus the promise of a whipping if we didn't do what we were told.

After a while some of us were set free and allowed to go out and settle the land as farmers. But we ran into a fair bit of resistance from these black people. They seemed to think that just because they'd lived in these parts all their lives the land was theirs. Strange, isn't it?

True, they had built some houses in certain places and they obviously knew their way around, but there were no cultivated fields, or factories or railway stations. Nothing except bush and the odd tree or rock that they thought was so important that they wouldn't let us cut them down or move them. And when we went fishing they complained if we caught more than one fish each and wanted to take the rest back home to sell.

Well, we had to clear that land if we wanted to get on ... so we ended up having huge fights with these people. We won most of them. Good thing we had guns I reckon.

Mind you it wasn't all that easy. Even when you'd

cleared your land there were problems. Some years it never rained and all the stock died out and farms turned into deserts. Some of us jumped and ran when we heard that gold had been discovered.

You beauty! A lot easier than farming it was. You just had to dig and dig and say your prayers and you'd be rich in no time. That's the good thing about mining of any kind really — all you have to do is find it and you're set for life.

But there were still some Blacks around the place. To get rid of them, we used to make up poison baits and leave them in creek beds. But we didn't manage to do them all, so after a while it was decided to round the rest up and put them in one place. We called these places reservations and while they were a bit like concentration camps the Germans had in the war, they were for their own good. Not to kill them you know, but to look after them.

It's incredible when you think about it. They reckon those Blacks lived out here for more than 40 000 years before we came along. They had their own languages, their own legal system, art, music — a pretty good life by the sounds of things. Everybody knew where they stood and it all came from the land and something they call the Dreaming.

But then they all started dying out and losing interest in what was going on. They were drinking and fighting, and getting all kinds of diseases. The food didn't agree with them either — white sugar and white flour — they didn't seem very happy at all.

Even when we brought in some builders from Canberra to design new houses and lives for them they weren't satisfied. And they didn't have one person, you know, one boss, who could speak for everybody, so it

11

was very difficult to get decisions out of them. Every time something important came up, everybody would get a say. Crikey! The conversations went on for weeks. That's no way to run a society! And then there were the special spiritual things which couldn't be changed. In their system, everybody is a part of the religious beliefs as well. It's very deep and goes back to the Creation and there are special stories about how things came to live and be in different places and every single person can trace his own life through these stories.

You've got no idea. It affects everything: laws, daily activities, family life ... and on top of that, they're all related to one another and look after each other if there's trouble.

They reckon that every person is also part of life around the place, like a tree or an animal or a river or whatever. And they reckon that God is alive and in these things as well, so they can't kill these things because it would be like killing themselves and God at the same time.

Crazy, isn't it? How can a country get ahead if the people in it have got ridiculous ideas like these? I don't know how they lasted as long as they did.

ADVERTISING

Advertising is an accepted part of Australian life. It is one of the largest industries in the country and it is everywhere. From balloons to billboards, throughout the media, anywhere a place can be found an ad will be placed.

One of the main jobs of the advertiser in this conflict between pleasure and guilt is not so much to sell the product as to give moral permission to have fun without guilt.

Ernest Dichter,
American Advertising Guru

What are we going to do about advertising? Ban it? Let it go unabated? More, we want more . . .? The shouts of different views are heard echoing up the Hume Highway past that dog on the tuckerbox, nearly fading altogether around Yass, then getting louder again as the final run into sin city via billboards, neon signs and car yards is made.

Advertising; the last refuge in a sorry world for creative and ambitious people who don't mind manipulation in the guise of a profession and who profit greatly by the great conundrum of our economic system. If we don't keep the big wheel turning and make sure that all that is produced is consumed, then as sure as night follows day, we'll all be ruined.

Or even worse, end up living in a totalitarian dictatorship where furniture, decent clothes, heating and colour are also banned, if the ad industry's' own advertisements are any guide. You know the ones — "They don't have advertising in some countries". Very powerful, very illogical — but that's advertising.

The genesis of modern advertising lies in the weapons and car manufacturers of America. At the end of World War II, the US economy was booming. America's industry, untouched by the conflict while the rest of the Western World had been reduced to rubble, needed somewhere to go.

The great consumer age was launched, propelled by the infant science of behavioural psychology. Commercials became the means of convincing people to buy things they didn't necessarily want or need. Bomb builders branched out into consumer durables, sometimes long-lasting, sometimes not. These were household items which every family could be persuaded that they could not do without — fridges, dishwashers, gramophones,

16

blenders, juicers, automatic garbage dispensers, electric knives, electric toothbrushes. All but the last item, due no doubt to a natural fear of short circuits on the tongue, soon became essential for the modern American home.

Meanwhile the car makers went to town. New models constantly appeared with a specific feature to guarantee turnover — ''built-in obsolescence'', meaning manufactured not to last. Raw materials were cheap, fuel unlimited and you weren't a good citizen of the great nation if there wasn't a fresh V8 in the garage every year.

Times have changed. The benign 50s have become the brittle 80s. The energy crisis, the pollution crisis, the economic crisis. We were still on our feet but only just. Fashion, perceptions and priorities changed. Some countries made cars that lasted a good deal longer than three years and yet the wheel kept turning and the ads kept coming. Convincing, persuading, bombarding, amusing and, of course, ultimately succeeding in making us spend — even when we really couldn't afford it.

Advertising is big business. Over 1.8 billion dollars was spent in one year in Australia convincing us that Meadow Lea is better than Eta, that we really did need a Toyota. Recent promises of a return trip for two to Hawaii, if we purchase within seven days, be quick, offer closes soon, hurry don't wait — blah, blah, blah — show how desperate salesmen have become.

Advertising is big business. The major part of advertising revenue is derived from the large corporations who run the world and service the kitchen. They are the only groups who can afford to pay for the flash hundred thousand dollar, 30-second mini movie and then shell out the extra $200 per second to get it on the magic box. Of course it's a free world and if you have a loose million sitting in your cheque account you could advertise daily

17

on television right around Australia just like the banks and the beer companies do.

To add insult to injury some of the multi-nationals who have a guaranteed market and regular profits and don't need to advertise do so anyway, just to build up the right kind of image with the public. The seal-loving petrol company is one of the many in this category.

Advertisers realise that information about the product or any kind of rational, reasoning approach will often fail dismally; the consumer can be rational as well and may choose to reject the argument, however well put. That is why sporting events and papal tours are so effective. It is far better to concentrate on our emotions, which are more easily manipulated.

Who could stop themselves reaching for the Kleenex when the infamous dial-home-to-grandmother-sitting-in-a-far-off-place Telecom ads were first shown?

Advertisers are clever. By using scientists to research the reasons and responses of consumers to various forms of stimuli the campaigns they present prey heavily on the hidden needs of people as distinct from actual needs.

Sex has been used to sell everything from trucks to flavoured milk.

One current ad featuring kids slinking about like sophisticates in a steamy disco is a good example. The target consumer, teenagers; the product, milk; the method of motivation, the very thing they spend a good deal of the day and night thinking and worrying about.

Selling a sense of power is another identified hidden need. Here is a recent example. Titled "Name your limit up to $20 000", the ad, for a credit card of course, featured the following lines, "You have the ability to take advantage of unexpected opportunities . . . solve personal cash flow problems at any time . . . the power to make important decisions without having to worry about finance . . ." and so on. Quick I need one, now. Who cares about interest rates and being in debt when you can be that kind of person.

The fact is that advertising is not neutral, not value free. It assists the devouring jaws of capitalism, it entices us with the most seductive images, the most exciting of ideas. It neither educates nor provides information and it favours the rich and the powerful who can afford to use it effectively.

In Australia most of the ad agencies have been bought out by the big American companies. The industry is self-regulated, which means that they make up their own rules.

Sports sponsorships have become the place where these advertisers go to reach the audience they wouldn't otherwise have. But they seem to be bending their rules a little. The alcoholic beverages code states that ". . . the content for advertisements for beer shall only be directed to adult audiences" (and the same applies to cigarette advertising) and that ads should "not feature people drinking alcohol before or while driving motor vehicles".

Where does that leave the audience of young people wat hing daring racing car drivers sweeping through the Marlboro corner in the Fosters Grand Prix, I wonder.

An industry which encourages non-rational responses, plays upon human weaknesses, exploits sexual sensitivities, creates an attitude of wastefulness towards national resources which, as Vance Packard pointed out thirty years ago in *The Hidden Persuaders*, has the power to do good or evil needs to be looked at long and hard.

Seen any good Buga Up ads lately?

AUSTRALIA

SHALL WE DANCE

Channel 10 television program —
Thursday evening, August 1987
    5.30 Perfect Match — Australian
        dating game
    6.00 News, Sport & Weather
    7.00 Neighbours — Australian
        soap opera
    7.30 Cheers — American situation
        comedy
    8.00 Nightcourt — American
        situation comedy
    8.30 LA Law — American drama
    9.30 Dallas — American soap
        opera
  10.30 Late News
  10.35 Superstars of Wrestling —
        American entertainment
        program
  11.35 Just Liz — British situation
        comedy

Australia's just a suburb of the USA — Chorus
of song performed by a 1970s rock band.

*You and I, your government and mine, your
country and mine share basic values and
principles.* Malcolm Fraser, PM, to Ronald
Reagan, US President, in 1981.

The Union Jack has been replaced by the Stars and Stripes, for Australia still does not have a flag of her own. We are a nation in name only; at heart we remain a colony. British customs, the rule of law and the primacy of Church and State have been superseded by the American alliance and the big corporation. The twin tidal waves of Hollywood and Madison Ave via the-world-according-to-the-Pentagon have left Australia gibbering and uncertain — an ineffective participant in the great drama that is the struggle of the people of the world to see peace and equity become a reality in their lives.

Do you remember the scene in the American film *Raiders Of The Lost Ark* where the hero, played by actor Harrison Ford, is engaged in hand to hand fighting with a horde of Arabian villains? He despatches all but one, a giant of a man who produces a two-edged sword which he twirls around his torso whilst waiting for the hero to respond. There's a brief moment whilst Ford contemplates finishing the fight by overpowering this giant, but instead, rather than disarm the brute with his already proven superior skill he saves himself the effort, pulls out a large revolver and shoots him dead.

This is the bomb culture at work, the American solution, which incidentally received the seal of approval from Australian audiences.

I recently witnessed the making of an international satellite link-up television programme between Australia and the US where the participants debated the topic "Science, Technology and the Future". Studio audiences in both countries were made up of college students who were required to vote on certain questions raised by the discussion.

Following one American expert's testimony about the huge amounts of money spent and the large numbers of scientists working in areas of military research in universities in America, the question was put whether students were (1) in favour of increasing spending on university research for military purposes and (2) in favour of university research for the Strategic Defence Initiative "Star Wars".

The Australian audience was amused when the American kids voted "no" for (1) and "yes" for (2). But laughter turned to cat-calls when the first advertisement on the screen showed two young United States Air Force pilots flashing about the skies in a supersonic jet fighter, then reaching into the on-board fridge for a quick Pepsi between missions.

The "now" generation was going about its everyday business.

Many Australians believe that the United States is our good friend and ally. Lots of us watch American TV shows, eat Big Macs, listen to American music, wear American fashions and adopt American traits. It is thought that the two countries share a common view of the world and that our interests are similar enough to justify describing the relationship between the two countries as "special".

But to what extent is this relationship reinforced by popular culture? I am not certain whether a definite answer can be given but it seems that American popular culture has all but emasculated its White Australian counterpart. Our views are becoming shaped according to their values and, whilst the American political tradition has aspects that deserve acknowledgement, it is the Sylvester Stallone vision that is working on the hearts and minds of the people in our country. This is wrong.

Of course there was an existing Australian culture that had survived intact longer than any other. But its

23

enormous scope and the quality of its existence was given little heed by the dominant technology of the British settlers.

Thus, the White cultural view reflected that of the Empire. God, King and Country became the catch cry as criminals and land takers struggled to reconcile European backgrounds with the rigours of settling the harsh Australian land. Once most of the Aborigines who resisted this view were overcome, the business of remaking the country began.

In time the seeds of a distinct White Australian culture emerged. Drawing inspiration from the experience of the bush, characterized by a streak of reckless independence coupled with support for your fellow mate as its positive qualities, and finding its expression in the poetry of Henry Lawson and the rebellion at Eureka, the ''Aussie'' experience was validated.

It began and ended there. By the age of the atom the urban Australian was a reality, the sunbronzed bushman a memory. As World War II took its course and the British Empire reached its swansong and threw its loyal colonies over in the process, we turned to the United States to rescue us from the Japanese. Any concern about the vulnerability of the great southern continent surrounded by millions of strangers was assuaged by the knowledge that our new big brother was there to back us up.

As we were saved so we in our gratitude embraced the Americans fully — their wars, their cars, their cigarettes and their international perspective, their movies and their presidents. When they wanted a place to put their spy stations we gladly gave it, when they needed cannon fodder we supplied it, when they wanted votes in the United Nations we delivered them.

The culture of Washington and Monroe tantalized and comforted us. This by itself was not such a bad thing for its foundations had been as complete an expression of free and democratic polity as Australians had witnessed.

And yet by embracing America without question we left a gap in our own cultural development. As the American dream went sour — Vietnam, Watergate, the poverty gap, and the largest budget deficit yet carried by a modern state shaking the eagles nest — so the culture which reinforced and reflected that decline, whilst often attempting to disguise the fall by fanfare, continues to subvert our own.

Even worse, without an Australian vision to compensate for the failure of the American dream to realise itself we have developed a culture centred on retrospection and cliché. This fails to satisfy us and leads to the feelings of despair and expressions of nihilism which surface as a reaction to false hope.

The domination of the vehicles of culture — television, movies, media, music — by small numbers of very rich and powerful persons and corporations means that authentic cultural expression struggles to find an outlet.

In the meantime, mega-capitalists and shameless politicians manipulate national sentiment through sporting events — the cheapest cultural experience — in order to stimulate a cultural identity so as to sell some particular brand of beer or variation of barren ideology.

In a world where change is constant, culture instant, where money rules OK?, where the contradictions of starving people on the news and the new brand of cat food on the ads is a constant reminder that we still haven't got it right, in this kind of world the last recourse for a culture which refuses to see the cracks in the mirror becomes fantasy.

So the movies that are made attempt to rewrite history. The good American always wins, the cop show shoot-out sees the gun as victor, violence is legitimized as entertainment and the "Star Wars" fantasy joins the list of humankind's perverse follies. Ronald Reagan's dream is a sick joke, while Martin Luther King's remains a necessity.

Meanwhile the video shops of every Australian town and suburb are well stocked with American propaganda, the toy shops have the latest weapons, and our own defence forces see nothing wrong with exercising with a nuclear navy whose military strategy is best summed up as shoot first and ask questions later.

This is not to say that there is nothing good that comes from Uncle Sam. I certainly prefer the freedom of that country to the state control of the other superpower, and there are substantial parts of the American cultural experience which are of value, their constitutional traditions for example. But we seem to take only the muck — the high-kitsch, credit card, liquor store, fast food, freeways, waterbeds and war comics world which exists in a vacuum because of our own failure to define and create something which reflects Australian values and aspirations.

It is unlikely that the fragile creation which is our world can be sustained without heeding the biblical injunction to love one another, or without a realistic assessment of what the needs of people are and how they might be met.

Where fantasy predominates nothing gets done, when the culture reflects the quality of hating our enemy the problems continue.

For Australians, the uncommon linking of our desire for security with the notion that it can be provided by a heavily armed powerful friend has neither the force of logic nor the understanding of the post Hiroshima age to sustain it. Rather this desire reflects a failure to reach an accommodation with the world and the region in which we live and the changes that have taken place around us. We have always looked through somebody else's glasses, it's time we saw clearly that our real purpose is to walk our own road.

The new Australian journey should lead to self-reliance, towards a state where equality rather than selfishness, conservation rather than consumption, dignity rather than domination and peace rather than war are the values and ambitions of its culture.

THE BUDGET

August 1986 saw Federal Treasurer Paul
Keating bring down a budget that was
designed to keep the country afloat
during harsh economic times. It
succeeded in alienating a large slab of
the Labor Party's traditional base with
the decision to resume uranium sales to
France in order to generate export
income of $66 million.

The King was in his counting house,
counting all his money.
The Queen was in the parlour,
eating bread and honey.

Budgets are boring. And this year's was no exception. But as well as heeding the hip-pocket nerve, the government's shopping list also provides a picture of the kind of state we're in. "We are in a mess."

It's a message that rang loudly through the corridors of power — the lucky country has become the anarchist fruit shop ... We are in a state of war ... We must tighten our belts ... adjust, make sacrifices ... SOS ...

Usually, the full meaning of the budget hits home when the price of your favourite vice goes up again. By that criteria, this year's model wasn't too bad. After all, how many spa-bath-using, wine-drinking, fast-foreign-car-driving factory workers do you know? That's right. None.

No doubt there are a few factory owners who fall into that category, but the fringe benefits tax will probably take care of them, (unless the Bob Ansett campaign against laws-that-you-don't-like-even-if-they-are-proper-and-legal succeeds, which it doesn't deserve to do).

Budgets are noisy, too. From the dull mumblings and intermittent hoonery of the bear pit of the House of Representatives while the speech is being read, through to the collective groans of business, unions and special interest groups of one sort or another, plus the empty rattle of the talk-back lines once the message has sunk in, the decibel level is always high.

The message, it seems, is that we are about to pay for living off the fat of the land for decades and decades. Fair enough. But who will actually be doing the paying, and for whom? And to what ends? These are the questions the budget doesn't really answer because it's caught in the basic conundrum of the modern industrialized state: how to manage the big lie.

The big lie is that governments can make the system

(as it is currently constituted) work. They can't. Consider the state of the poor people in Australia whose numbers are growing daily. According to the Australian Consumers Association low income earners are going into debt to pay for essential household services. And that debt figure is getting higher. Fifty three per cent of the total consumer debt money is owed on personal bank loans and credit cards.

This compares with a national ten per cent that Australia owes in debt interest to overseas banks. As a nation we use our money to buy F-18 fighters and French champagne. The poor use theirs to buy bread.

So long as governments are required to operate the financial affairs of the nation with the underlying premise of sustained economic growth as one of the holy writs of society, then the contradictions of capitalism will jump out from the pages of documents like the Budget.

The first of these relates to the participation in the national economy of free marketeers who have a degree of profit as their prime motivation. Mr Keating called on all Australians to invest more and consume less, but if we examine the level of private money invested through institutions — banks, superannuation funds, trusts and so on — we discover that the amount that has been sent overseas has increased dramatically in recent years and currently stands at 7 billion dollars.

One would think that, if things are as bad as everybody makes out, this money could be put to better use in our country. What's more, the people who make the profits get considerable taxation advantages as well. How many of our leading superannuation funds are involved in this business? Most of them — to the great detriment of our nation.

Secondly, trade is seen as the path to real

independence. This is an even more incredible claim if you consider the recent developments in the United States where mid-western farmers' wheat is being sold at bargain basement prices to the Russians while the best response our own beleagured rural lobby can muster is to dump a few bushels on the steps of Parliament House.

Thirdly, we should look at who is actually paying the tax and what they're getting for it. Contrary to popular opinion, Australians are not the highest taxpayers in the world — in fact, we sit about half way down the list of Western countries. However, under our present system it's Jane and Bill Average, the normal wage or salary earners, who pay most of the tax and their contribution is getting larger every year (around 43% of tax in 79/80 up to 63% in 83/84). At the same time, the tax paid by companies has decreased accordingly (around 18% in 79/80 down to 14% in 83/84). The 600 million dollar man, Mr Robert Holmes a' Court, even gets tax concessions to carry on his business of asset acquisition. Profits are high.

But it is in relation to matters of principle that this budget sets the seal on what the present government has become: the natural successor to the Liberal–National Party coalition as the conservative ruler of Australia. When a budget speech can be used to overturn party policy, then any pretence of democratic decision-making is finished.

Flying in the face of ALP policy which specifically states that the government should work towards providing an increase in foreign aid to those Third World neighbours in need, the Hawke government significantly reduced that foreign aid.

Their decision to resume uranium sales to France goes against the grain of another plank in the ALP platform which specifically states that Australian yellow cake should not be made available to the nuclear terrorists whose behaviour we've been complaining about for the past decade. It's only a matter of time before the huge concrete plug that holds Muroroa Atoll together dissolves and the east coast of Australia sees the return of the bi-products of that uranium in the form of severe radiation poisoning.

Any claims to being the party of the people, a force for peace and disarmament in our region, or even responsible to its own decision making bodies can now be seen for what they are — the hollow shams of those more interested in the politics of power than the long-term future of the nation.

There are singular myths that flow through the blood-streams of society. They are used to justify, obscure or explain why things happen the way they do. Myth manipulation is currently alive and well in our world — and is generally perpetuated by the rich and powerful to control the many who are poor.

In England, the class system that arose during the period of Britain's expansion remains intact through the myth of the Empire which is now kept alive only through royal weddings and wars.

In Australia, the myth of the equal society that once found an expression in our national consciousness is perpetuated by those who claim to represent the many, but more often than not appear to be serving the few.

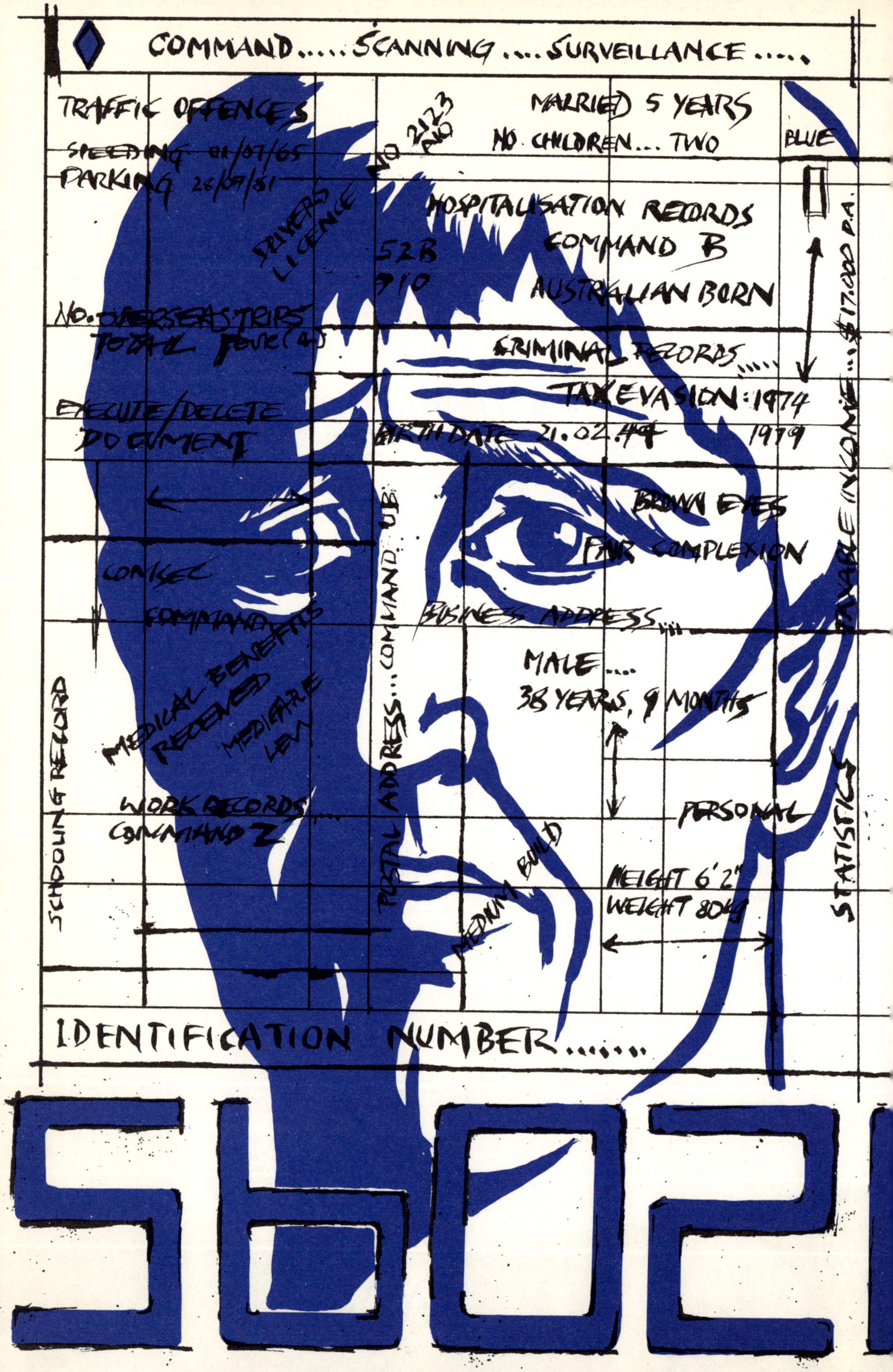

COMMAND..... SCANNING .... SURVEILLANCE .....

TRAFFIC OFFENCES

SPEEDING 01/07/65
PARKING 26/09/81

NO. 2123
NO

MARRIED 5 YEARS
NO. CHILDREN... TWO

BLUE

DRIVERS
LICENCE

52B
910

HOSPITALISATION RECORDS
COMMAND B
AUSTRALIAN BORN

NO. OVERSEAS TRIPS
TOTAL FOUR (4)

CRIMINAL RECORDS.....
TAX EVASION: 1974
1979

EXECUTE/DELETE
DOCUMENT

BIRTH DATE 21.02.44

BROWN EYES
FAIR COMPLEXION

COMSEC

COMMAND

BUSINESS ADDRESS...

MALE....
38 YEARS, 9 MONTHS

MEDICAL BENEFITS
RECEIVED

MEDICARE
LEVY

SCHOOLING RECORD

POSTAL ADDRESS.... COMMAND. UB.

TAXABLE INCOME... $17,000 P.A.

WORK RECORDS
COMMAND Z

PERSONAL

MEDIUM BUILD

HEIGHT 6'2"
WEIGHT 80kg

STATISTICS

IDENTIFICATION NUMBER.......

THE AUSTRALIA CARD

In 1986 the federal ALP government introduced its controversial Australia Card legislation, paving the way for a national register of all Australian citizens and the provision of individual identification cards. Upon its first presentation, the legislation was rejected by the Senate. This process was repeated, thus providing the trigger for a double dissolution and subsequent election which was called to provide the government with a sufficient majority to make the ID card law.

I feel like a number, I feel like a number. Bob Seger
I'm an individual. Jacko

Things are moving too quickly around here. We are in deep trouble. The alarm bells are ringing loudly. Can anybody hear them? George Orwell was only two years out. Oceania is to be the starting point and, disguised as public servants from the Department of Health, the thought police are ready to do their stuff.

Some time ago, the federal government set up a committee comprising representatives from all political parties to examine the repercussions of the proposed national identification card. After much deliberation, the majority of the committee members concluded that the card should not be introduced, it would not work, it would cost too much to run, and it would seriously affect our civil liberties.

Cabinet and caucus have ignored the recommendation. The government still wants to introduce the card. *Hmmm.*

Imagine a future where thousands of public servants from various government departments, employers, police and any other corporation or person who has gained access to a national identification number of John Citizen (whether legally or illegally) will be able to identify and follow every single activity John has undertaken in the past.

Where you lived, where you worked, number of traffic offences, last time in hospital, length of time receiving unemployment benefits, what you bought at the supermarket, last time you visited a counsellor, what motel you stayed in when you visited Melbourne, what you said when you called up your friends to complain that Hunters and Collectors weren't playing in town and so on and so on.

I am not exaggerating. A leading computer expert described the ID card proposal as ". . . a scheme to create a centralized government databank on every Australian''. Now that's what I call heavy.

The scheme is designed to allow integration of data presently held by different agencies for different purposes. This process is called computer matching, and by giving each Australian an identification number, it provides a key to the system whereby the personal details of each of us are stored in one central data bank, a data bank that's made up of a number of computer systems.

Such a system cannot be set up so as to guarantee safety. You may be unable to get a job because there could be incorrect information in the system saying that in the past you were fired for stealing from the till.

Keyboard error, blackmail, vandalism, commercial usages and hackers having fun are all potential threats to the security and integrity of such a system. Remember the home computer operators who tapped into the Pentagon system?

The material on your file could be delivered by a third party, so you may not even know the reason that you were knocked back for the job, what the information was or where it came from. Once an error is in the system it is virtually undetectable, and in the government's legislation there are no provisions for compensation if it's the system that makes the mistake.

The system could be used to track people down. Take the example of a woman trying to escape from a violent boyfriend whose brother works in the Department of Immigration and thus has access to the system. Although the woman has changed her address, every time she has any kind of dealing with a government department or agency she can be traced to her new location, and guess who's waiting for her when she comes home?

The proposed ID card is a completely unacceptable and outrageous invasion of our privacy. To be handed over to the whim of a computer and a public servant is bad enough, but when you think about the possibilities of abuse under such a scheme, we need to protest long and loud.

The ID card will be more than a piece of plastic with your photo on it. It will be a national citizens registration scheme based on a central register which, in time, would develop into a mass surveillance system of all Australians.

There is not one single national identification scheme in the world that operates satisfactorily. Drug smugglers in the United States are routinely found with half a dozen social security numbers. The Swedish system has produced a burgeoning black market and efforts to strengthen the system such as the proposed ID card here were knocked back by the public because of the fear of abuse. In Canada, you need to produce your number to borrow a library book. In Germany the system is detested.

At the guts of all this is the unavoidable fact that governments of either persuasion cannot be absolutely trusted. Such a system, if introduced, would produce one of the tightest social security nets in the world. And what guarantees do we have that the net will not be widened or tampered with in the future?

In a letter to the *Age*, 18/7/85, citizen no. 6934718, Dr Neil Blewett, stated that,

> Name, sex, date of birth, and identifying number, is all the information which would be included in the Australian card register.

Yet interdepartmental communications leaked to the media, author presumed to be citizen 6934718, stated,

Only less sensitive data are to be held in a system initially, with the facility to input at a later stage when public acceptance maybe forthcoming more readily.

Sensitive data? What are they talking about? What does *sensitive* mean?

I'd recommend sending Dr Blewett a copy of *1984*. Make sure you include his identification number otherwise he may not read it. Then write a letter to your Democrat or Liberal Party senator. The ID card legislation must not be passed.

We have seen the future and we do not want it to be like this.

Postscript

The Australian Computer Society in a public statement on 4 November 1986 said that "... consideration of the Australia Card proposal should be *deferred* until after the long-promised privacy protections have been enacted, and a privacy protection scheme has been firmly established".

KAKADU

In September 1985, Prime Minister
Hawke wrote to his Environment
Minister expressing concern about the
lack of a mangement plan for Kakadu
National Park with "any provision for the
possible future recovery of minerals
within the park". The subsequent release
of the letter provoked a public outcry
and further tremblings of revolt from
within the Labor Party. All this at a time
when that same government was
recommending the region for a World
Heritage listing, meaning that the area
was of such critical important to the
planet that it should never be tampered
with.

*Man did not weave the web of life, he is
merely a strand in it. Whatever he does to the
web he does to himself.*

Chief Seattle, 1853

In this, the year of the broken promise, "Let's Create Instead of Rape" should be the new slogan for the recently launched Buy Australian campaign.

Instead, the federal government — with a commitment to the protection of National Parks as an unchallengeable plank in its party platform — is considering allowing mining in Kakadu.

It seems as though we have very short memories. In the early 80s our political leaders foresaw Australia becoming rich through the biggest mining boom the world had ever seen. Money was borrowed, equipment bought, holidays planned and the country, with Prime Minister Fraser at the helm, prepared itself for the golden decade. It never arrived.

Today, commodity prices for uranium, platinum and most other precious metals that we have a bountiful supply of, are way down. Mines around the country are operating at half steam and the interest bill on the money borrowed to finance the big killing is rising and adding to our national debt.

Faced with this reality, what better way to ensure that *if* and when the market price goes up we have more than enough to sell, than to make the idea of World Heritage meaningless by letting the miners into one of the most amazing pieces of unspoilt land that remains on the earth today?

Words cannot express the beauty and the depth of Kakadu. Before visiting it in August '86, I had never seen such an extraordinary variety of bird and animal life in one place. It is a nature documentary in real life; great beauty abounds. The park contains the greatest prehistoric art gallery in the world with cave paintings that were begun 230 centuries before Christ walked out from Galilee.

And then there's the land forms of stone plateaus, coastal plains and lowlands populated by an astonishing variety of plants and native flowers — about 1500 species all up — some of which are still unnamed. It's one of Australia's greatest assets, a place for all Australians to visit and appreciate, a region with extraordinary tourist potential.

The whole area is owned by the Aboriginal people who have leased it back to the Australian National Parks and Wildlife Service so that it can be protected for all to enjoy. But now the miners want to dig out the only metal that has a current value in the world, gold, a move that could threaten the most precious habitat we have.

The decision to limit mining to the proposed Stage 3 of the park is completely at odds with the greater needs of the Kakadu area. The mining sites are situated at the headwaters of the South Alligator River. Because the South Alligator flows into areas of the park that have already been proclaimed, the risks of accidental contamination are high.

One tonne of ore — about a Holden Commodore's worth — would, after processing, give the miner about two grams of gold. The remainder of the rock, pulverised into a fine dust, would be disposed of in the middle of the nature reserve. And this in an area of nine different ecosystems with a predominance of woodland, a rarity in the Top End.

There is no doubt that the activities of the mining industry with its associated resource use and consequent pollution would affect Stages 1 and 2 of the park. So when are we going to stop and consider the consequences of the ''dig-it-all-out-and-sell-it-now'' approach to development?

Of course, we must properly utilise our natural

43

resources in order to develop the country further. But why use it just as a quarry? Don't we need to process and produce other items instead of just loading the country into a truck and picking up a cheque at the end of the day? Can't we understand that our national estate is an even more precious resource in a world losing forests, plant and animal species — indeed the complete web of genetic diversity that makes up the ecosphere — at a daily rate? Apparently not.

The Daintree forest in Queensland is the only complete rainforest ecosystem region left in the country. Over the past one million years it has produced most of the existing plant species that are on planet earth. And yet the Queensland government, in its bid for progress at any cost, has allowed its subdivision and destruction. Further north, the Queensland government seems determined to give over the entire Cape York region to mining, tourist development and, no doubt, special landing strips for bomb-laden B-52s.

In New South Wales, the wetlands of Botany Bay — birthplace of European Australia — are to be the site of a multi-national's chemical factory.

In Victoria, the woodchipping companies will reduce the great forests of East Gippsland to pulp in order to satisfy the insatiable demand for greeting cards and coloured toilet paper.

And so it goes on . . .

Scientists believe that the right-hand-side of the brain is the creative, emotional and visual part of the organ, while the left-hand-side is that which controls the rational and thus spurs our materialistic instincts. So perhaps we need a right-hand-side-of-the-brain movement to take over the politics of Oz while we leave the left-hand-siders out in the back paddock for a while.

When it comes to the warfare known as mining, apart from providing for proper protection of our precious environment, perhaps the first right-hand-side action could be to reinstate the notion of a resources tax, with a special provision that the monies be paid into a commonwealth fund to be used for the purpose of developing the artistic output of Australians — music, art, fashion, literature. With videos of real nature zones as an additional purchasing incentive, such a scheme would provide an addition to our export industries that our balance of payments desperately needs. It's either that or uranium, by the looks of things.

We come from a land down under, where women glow and men plunder. Can you hear? Can you hear the thunder? You'd better run, you'd better take cover.

Postscript

When Prime Minister Hawke, in an effort to win back the conservation vote, visited Kakadu in November 1986 he said it would be "an obscenity" to mine there. But because of opposition from the Northern Territory government and the mining giants, his bid to have the region declared a World Heritage area was postponed. In a recent Federal Court battle, the mining companies won the right to explore for minerals in the park.

REYKJAVIK SUMMIT

In early October, US President Ronald
Reagan and Soviet leader Mikhail
Gorbachev met in Reykjavik, Iceland, for
a series of talks on arms control. Massive
reductions in the number of nuclear
weapons held by each side were
proposed, but negotiations broke down
with President Reagan's refusal to limit
his Strategic Defence Initiative research
to the laboratory. At the conclusion of
the meeting, Mr Gorbachev appealed to
America, saying, "Let America think. We
are waiting. We are not withdrawing our
proposals."

All the world's a stage,
And all the men and women merely players:
They have their exits and their entrances;
And one man in his time plays many parts...

William Shakespeare

A great drama is in the process of being played out before the world. It's called *Will We, Or Won't We?* and the leading players are two giants. Both of them are inclined to the view that might is right. Both are aware that should they fight then everything, including their natural habitat, would be destroyed.

The drama has been running for many lifetimes, but has recently experienced a new development: The Final Act. At this point, the puppets in the play — one, a real-life actor, the other a bureaucrat — are struggling. They have different local support groups, but a universal audience; they have different scriptwriters, but the story remains the same; they have similar ambitions, but conflicting solutions. They've just returned from playing a scene in Iceland where many words were spoken but little was achieved.

The Icelandic scene was titled "Arms Control" although it could have been called "Public Opinion Control". The dialogue in the scene included promises to relieve world anxiety through the largest reductions in nuclear weapons ever proposed by the superpowers, Russia and America.

But at the end of the day there was nothing. The meeting between the bosses of the superpowers was a dismal failure. As with the hundreds of other discussions that have taken place, there was a sticking point. This time it was called "Star Wars".

Star Wars is the "Strategic Defence Initiative", a plan that involves putting weapons (some of which are fuelled by nuclear explosions) into space to provide a complete defence against enemy warheads. It is a dream of President Reagan's which is as flawed as the logic which speaks of winning nuclear wars.

A majority of scientists are convinced that SDI, as it

is known, will not work. Involving revolving mirrors suspended in the stratosphere, satellites which fire rockets, particle beam generators and so on, all of which are to be co-ordinated and executed by one enormous computer programme that's never been tested, its highly complex series of defence layers is a guaranteed statistical failure.

Once it's put into practice, research for the programme will breach one of the few treaties that the Soviets and the Americans have generally managed to observe: the Anti-Ballistic Missile Treaty of 1972.

The programme is very expensive. $1.6 trillion by 1990.

In 1953, former American president Dwight D. Eisenhower observed that,

> Every gun that is made, every warship launched, every rocket fired, signifies in a final sense a theft from those who hunger and are not fed — those who are cold and not clothed.

But the truth of that statement is often obscured by the rattling of hi-tech swords and the media focus on the action of the puppets rather than the consequences of their decisions.

In order to pay for the fantasy of a nuclear shield in space, the Americans need to borrow. And so the economies — ours, theirs and the Third World's — all suffer. Of course, the Soviets must respond, diverting more resources to the military in order to match the Americans. As famine crushes Africa and the basic human necessities of fresh water, food and shelter are denied to millions, the arms race heads into space.

It has been argued that an agreement with the Soviet

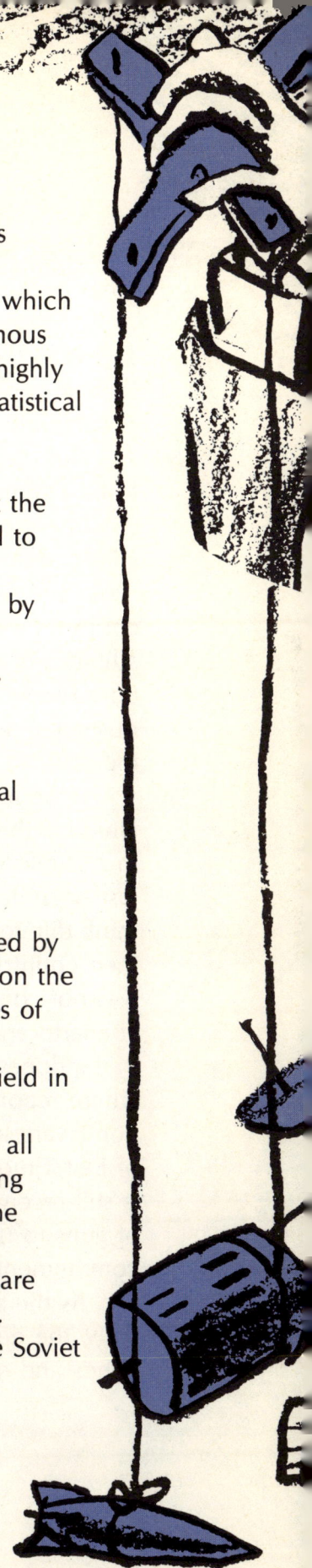

49

Union on disarmament is conditional upon an improvement in human rights in that country.

As a member of Amnesty International, I have protested the treatment given to individuals in the Russian peace movement. Totalitarianism, wherever it occurs, must be deplored.

But the West's concern about human rights appears to be conditional. Australian business people (including the Treasurer of the Liberal Party, Mr John "Fosters" Elliott) seek profit by trading with the Russians. Surely trade, the most fundamental of relations between countries, needs also to be undertaken with our moral attitudes in mind. Not so, it seems, as the Americans dump tonnes of wheat into Soviet kitchens while Australian farmers — free world allies to a man — go to the wall.

It would be a mistake to believe that the Soviet Union is the sole repository of evil in the modern world. In Australia's front yard, nine elderly communists have just been executed in Indonesia because they happen to think differently from the military government which runs their country. Apparently a twenty year stretch in prison was not considered sufficient punishment by General Soeharto and company.

Indonesia: where press censorship is commonplace; where reports of the torture and indiscriminate killing of non-Javanese (particularly those in the conquered territory of East Timor) continue to filter out; where Australian aid is still received ... What price can we put on the export of guns to Indonesia, I wonder, in view of our so-called commitment to human rights?

As the schoolchildren of Soweto are shot and gaoled daily, the democratic nations of the world sit on their hands and make noises about Apartheid. For our efforts,

we've managed to reduce the amount of aid given to those African countries currently being squashed by the racist South African regime of thugs and bully boys. Our only contribution to the application of pressure on the South African regime is to stop QANTAS flying to Johannesburg plus the production of a voluntary code for Australian companies suggesting they don't do business with the Apartheid regime, which is ignored by many. It's not much of a commitment to human rights, is it?

At the heart of President Reagan's refusal to sacrifice Star Wars is the fact that the program has nothing to do with the non-nuclear defence that he speaks so highly of. Nor is the issue of American freedom central to the discussion. Rather, it is a continuation of the strategy that has underpinned US foreign policy from the word go and which has been expressed as the ability of American forces to "prevail" in any conflict with the Soviet Union.

When the goal of SDI is summed up by America's Assistant Director of Defence as

> not the defence of the nation as a whole, not of every city and person in it, but the defence of America's capability to retaliate,

then we understand why President Reagan is so determined to hang on, and why Mr Gorbachev is so afraid.

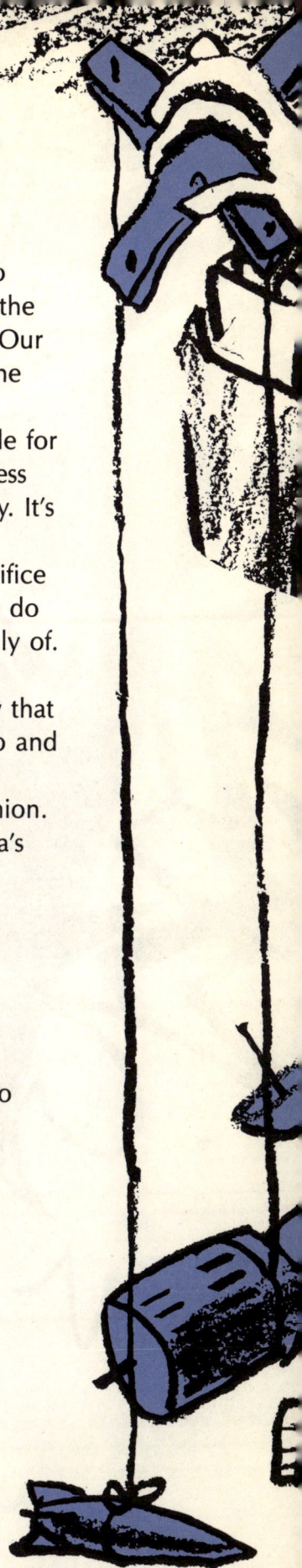

VISITS BY NUCLEAR-ARMED SHIPS

When the Royal Australian Navy celebrated its seventy-five years of nuclear-free defence in October '86, Sydney harbour was visited by a fleet of forty warships from the navies of seven countries. Among them were six British and United States vessels suspected of carrying nuclear weapons.

There is no sin but ignorance.

Marlowe 1564

It's a birthday party with a difference.

Instead of a cake, we have Prince Philip and a fireworks display.

The guests roll up in a million tonnes of floating armour. They've got helicopters, jump-jets and a battalion of marines. Some of them have, at their disposal, an arsenal of nuclear depth charges and nuclear missiles.

The venue for their party is a port with a population of four million people.

Set out below is a record of the day's events.

5am: He wakes after a restless night's sleep. It's dark and drizzling with rain. Already, the largest collection of warships ever assembled off the east coast is preparing to make its entrance through the Heads.

He pulls out the phone book to check the number for Boating Weather Information. "Typical," he mumbles as a large destroyer looms up from the cover, "even Telecom's getting into the act. Next it'll be recorded messages like

> 'Two nuclear armed naval vessels collided in slight seas off the Opera House this morning. Do not panic. Have a nice day'."

He glances at the morning paper to see if anything important has happened. A report of the Grand Final begins

> Rugby League is sometimes like what we expect of nuclear war. It leaves survivors rather than victors.

Survivors for what? he thinks.

By the time he gets down to Rose Bay on the Harbour shore, people are already preparing the peace fleet for the day's activities. Some have slept on their boats overnight. People are rigging sails, checking canoes and kayaks and clambering into wetsuits. There's a barge, some large yachts and a number of motor boats . . . There must be about fifty craft, he reckons. Not bad for a rainy Monday morning.

The peace fleet has been practising for weeks. Everybody is aware that being on the harbour with seven navies, the water police, various tugs and the New Right isn't going to be easy. People are careful to follow the guidelines set down by the organisers.

Of course, there will be a couple of brave souls who'll swim in front of the nuclear-armed ships and hang onto the bow. Great courage for a great photo. People call them ratbags. It's incredible, isn't it, that people who are prepared to risk their lives for a cause are called names?

Out on the water, there are boats everywhere. It's not that easy keeping afloat in a canoe when you're up against wind and rain, choppy seas and the churning of high speed motor boats, but everybody seems to manage.

"Here they come!" Huge thrusting grey steel mountains charge down the harbour. "There's one of ours!" Everybody cheers. seventy-five years of nuclear-free defence. "Good on you!" Don't like the look of the American ship behind, though. It carries nuclear weapons. It's travelling very fast. "Who's the ratbag around here?" he wonders.

Eighteen hours earlier, a retired naval officer who'd been in charge of port safety in Western Australia had explained why he resigned. His name was Lieutenant Commander Michael Lynch and in a media briefing he said, "There are absolutely no plans, no procedures, no precautions and no policies to deal with accidents [involving nuclear weapons]."

Most states do not have a port safety plan that looks at weapons accidents. Victoria and New South Wales fall into this category. Others — Tasmania and the Northern Territory — say they've got a plan, but no one is allowed to see it. Instead, they ignore the potentially catastrophic situation in the same way that the nuclear powers do with their "neither confirm nor deny" nonsense.

As if any ship is going to turn around and sail half

way across the world to pick up its ammunition when times of hostility arise — everybody knows that the ships carry their atomic weapons with them.

That's why there were people on the water.

Still, the action has been a good one. No one was hurt, there was only one arrest, and the media was everywhere: looking for blood, it seemed.

By the time he gets his canoe out of the water and drives home, the evening news is on. Unbelievably, all they show is a few shots of paddlers and surfers, plus pro-nuclear American yachts. There are no pictures of the majority of the peace fleet, nor is there any mention of why people felt it was important to demonstrate. Nor was there any mention of the fact that the anti-nuclear people far out-numbered the Liberals.

"You can't believe a thing you see on telly, these days", he thinks. "Someone should complain about it." But he's too tired at the moment, so he decides to watch Four Corners and then crash.

The Four Corners team are doing a story on the ships. During the course of the program, they interview an Australian admiral. He says that accidents won't happen while the ships are in port.

"What about US Navy records of 381 accidents involving nuclear weapons?" asks the interviewer.

"Well, the Americans practise for accidents all the time," says the admiral.

But as the program explains, the last nuclear weapons accident practice was held in 1983. The next one isn't due to take place until 1989. And in any event, if the nukes are in other people's harbours, then the practice is meant to take place there . . . Let's evacuate the entire population of Sydney's eastern suburbs in an hour and a half, gang!

56

To round it off, Four Corners reminds us that the US government is not prepared to accept liability in the case of a nuclear weapons accident. As well as this, the US government has a policy which stipulates the creation of a special national defence area around any accident site which would be off-limits to all Australians (including the navy, the police and the Prime Minister) until further notice.

He felt a little better about his day on the water. "If the Americans won't accept responsibility, and Australian governments won't accept responsibility," he thought, "that leaves the people to do the job."

It leaves the people to do the job because nuclear weapons on the ships of other nations pose the most serious threat to the safety of all the people living in the cities in which those ships are berthed; because they *are* nuclear targets, because they *can* have accidents, and because there are *no* plans to deal with anything going wrong. So the only proper response is for people to work to prevent those ships from coming in.

"I'll be out on the water again," he said to himself.

During a series of Nuclear Weapons Accident Exercises in Nevada in 1981, soldiers acting as demonstrators at the site broke through the security cordon. The official report states,

> *It was simulated that one demonstrator was shot.*

HAWKE v. LANGE

Since the election of Bob Hawke in
1982 and David Lange in 1983, Australia
and New Zealand have been governed
by political parties which share the same
label. Trade between the nations has
increased and in some policy areas, such
as deregulation of the economy, a
shared perspective is evident. On the
question of relations with the United
States, in particular its nuclear weapons
policies, the leaders of the two countries
have embarked upon very different
paths.

*For whosoever exalteth himself shall be
abased; and he that humbleth himself shall be
exalted.*

Luke 14:11

If the superpowers and their leaders who threaten our existence believe they can play God and if our own leaders don't believe that God exists, then who is actually ordering the affairs of the world, I wonder.

Faced with the increasing decline in the ability of the established church to gather and invigorate our belief, some in the West are looking eastwards for spiritual salvation, and in turn they end up looking at themselves.

These new trans-personal philosophies posit a view of a God within us that relates to the whole universe. Like Nietzcshe, the tragic German philosopher who called up the Anti-Christ, the new philosophy in its boldest forms proclaims men as gods.

A quick glance at our current bosses should convince anyone that we are ruled by plain-as-day mortals. While we might expect our leaders to behave in a manner fitting their position there is no earthly reason why they, along with the rest of us, should be able to lead perfect lives. But, unlike the average person, our leaders do make decisions that have important consequences for all of us.

After placing themselves in the public gallery and saying, "Trust me. I'll do the right thing," their actions are henceforth judged by the wider world and their motivations and ideals subject to our attention.

Which brings us to New Zealand, the land of 3.2 million people, where milk bars are called dairies, rugby is the state religion and a large ex-lawyer and lay preacher called David Lange, the Prime Minister.

Aoteoroa, the land of the long white cloud, shares some qualities with its most important neighbour, Australia. Like us the White settlers had to contend with the local people before the European take-over was complete. But the settlers there saw fit to negotiate the

Treaty of Waitangi with the Maoris in the 1840s, something we haven't got around to yet.

Similarly, both countries were loyal outposts of the British Empire, providing men and raw materials of wool, wheat and dairy produce to the industrial nations of Europe. Both established Westminster style parliamentary government although New Zealand was not cursed by states, being content like most sensible democracies to allow national governments to do just that, govern the nation.

Their political parties are similar to ours, although New Zealand on occasion has spawned strange entities difficult to classify by normal standards. What are we to make, for example, of a free enterprise anti-nuclear political party? There was such a thing in the last NZ election.

We enjoy the same sports although Kiwis, understandably, took a dim view of the Greg Chappell underarm bowling incident, and our reputation as a nation of fair-minded, fair dinkum types suffered. Kiwis are proud people and their considerable achievements in building a society where the poor and down-trodden are adequately protected was the standard by which other social welfare systems were judged.

Indefatigable travellers, many Australians and New Zealanders backpack the world seeking a broader vista to make sense of their own homeland. While Aussies flock to London a lot of young New Zealanders lured by the bright lights and high wages of the big smoke come to Australia in search of greater things; many stay.

Mr Hawke and Mr Lange both travelled to England when young, Mr Hawke to study at Oxford, Mr Lange to work in London as a lawyer.

Their experiences abroad were markedly different.

Mr Hawke, we are told by his biographer, Blanche d'Alpuget, spent much of the time "drinking and womanising" while Mr Lange ended up at a place called the West London Mission where he was greatly influenced by the ideas of one of the regular preachers there, a Lord Soper who believed that socialism is the expression of that part of the Christian ethic which properly has to do with politics and economics. The mission took in vagrants from around the London area, and Mr Lange along with other volunteers would look after them. Mr Hawke's mentors included such diverse people as academics, trade union officials and, later on in life, senior businessmen from the other side of the political fence.

Both men worked intensely in their chosen fields and were relatively late arrivals into politics. Lange as a people's lawyer in Auckland represented the poor and itinerant, often in the lower courts, while Hawke became the voice of the trade union movement in Australia, loved by his constituency, the working Aussie, and respected by those against whom he was arguing.

Both came from religious backgrounds, although Mr Hawke early on renounced his faith, and both sought to ameliorate a particular physical condition upon seeking the highest political office in the land. In Lange's case a stomach stapling operation saw his weight reduced to manageable proportions; Mr Hawke forswore the grog.

Both leaders lay great emphasis on consensus but differ on the question of ambition. According to Mr Lange, "an ambition makes you a pretty ordinary person". Mr Hawke's views on this matter are well known. Both are fortunate in being in partnership with outstanding and supportive women. Mrs Lange was reluctant to move into the Prime Ministerial residence when her husband was elected and suggested that it be used as an orphanage. All Australians, quite rightly, admire the warm and sensible Hazel Hawke.

Yet Mr Lange is well loved by his countrypeople, listened to overseas, and considered a leader of stature in world affairs, while Mr Hawke is not. Part of this relates to the differing policies of the two countries. New Zealand has taken the step, begun the process of untangling itself from the nuclear world and at the same time working in its local region to advance the causes of peace and justice.

The mere presence of a leader from however small a nation speaking up for the hopes of millions of people and clearly advocating the wishes of his own is bound to attract notice and respect. The same cannot be said of our leader who chooses merely to represent the policies of a superpower, whether from fear or ignorance we know not.

New Zealand came of age in the oil crisis of the early 70s. Self-reliance and active engagement in world affairs within its own sphere of influence have become features of the Kiwi state. We, on the other hand, neither sovereign nor satellite, continue as before, unaware it seems that the world is a changed place and unable to recognise our own strength and our potential to make something (good) of what we are.

In 1973 Mr Hawke led the fight in international forums against French testing in the Pacific; in 1986 as Prime Minister he was prepared to let us sell them the raw material of nuclear weapons so that very nation could continue this activity. Mr Hawke was suggesting to his Environment Minister that mining could be allowed in the Kakadu National Estate. Now he believes that mining should not be allowed, and so it goes on.

63

Is it true that the spirit of the nation is reflected in the leaders it elects to govern it? Australians are in need of a future vision which a leader will speak about and act upon.

The sorry spectacle of half-truths and circumlocutions, that emanate from our Prime Minister's mouth compares poorly with the straightforward behaviour of the New Zealand Prime Minister, Mr Lange, and provides little comfort for those of us who believe that for leaders to be followed they must be trusted.

State Transition.
1 of the relation to the Imperial
clusion of the Armed forces is
whole of the

(s

(ii) ritorial limits

ations (s 51 (v

countries and an
1 excise) (s 51 (ii),

of p

TATED CONSTITUTION

espect to mers relating to any dep
to make laws constitution nsferred to the Comn
1 of which is the military fs and postal services
clude contr ng duties ooms and excise and
ake law respect to Commwealth territc

Common falling withi

inage (s 1 1
ntain milit es for the c

Comm fal

lit

Imperial po
xviii)). 29
dental to the exer
nt (and officers), and

RENT POWERS

This leaves a large
nt power
mmerce with other
(apart from customs a
etc (s.51 (vii)). 30
1 and meteorolog
51 (ix)).
istralian wate
tistics (s 51
xiii)).

CONSTITUTIONAL COMMISSION

Proclaimed in 1901, Australia's Constitution is seen by many as an outdated document that lacks the flexibility to change with the times. For many years, people have expressed a desire to change the Constitution, to make it more relevant in a changing world. But it wasn't until July 1986 that the federal government set up a committee to examine the document and take submissions from the public on how it should be changed. Peter Garrett was among committee members chosen to advise and perhaps amend the document. Proposed changes to the Constitution will be put to the people of Australia in a series of referendums in 1988.

All men are equal, but some are more equal than others.

George Orwell

It is all but invisible to the naked eye. It cannot be easily digested. It is a product of history and the result of compromise. It reflects a bit of England, a bit of America and a bit in between.

It is said to be alive, although it has hardly breathed in the past eighty years of its existence. It is the central most important foundation upon which the country sits and yet no school kids could tell you what's in it. It is the plot behind the drama of government in Australia and yet it does not mention any of the leading players.

Could we please introduce the Australian Constitution — *Zzzz, snore, zzz.*

George Washington, the honest president, believed that states should have revolutions every seventeen years in order to stop democracy from going stale. In the current period of domestic malaise and international trauma there is a possibility that we the people could engender our own peaceful and productive revolution in 1988.

Cheaper than the Bicentenary and more significant than the America's Cup, it's the Constitutional Commission. For the first time in our history, a process of constitutional review has been undertaken. It is directed by and through the wider community and allows all Australians to participate by giving opinions about change through submissions and public hearings and finally by casting their votes by way of referendum.

By the end of the last century, it was clear that after a mere hundred years of European settlement, the six colonies which inhabited the greater land mass of Australia were born to squabble. Despite deriving their political structures from the same source, they could agree on little. In time, different border taxes, different railway gauges and the threat of separate armies encroached on the future vision of the colonists.

Growing concern about the threat of French and German expansion into the Pacific and New Guinea regions alarmed the states into agreeing to join together as one. Meetings were held and speeches made. Partly modelled on the American Constitution (without the Bill of Rights) and partly on the British Constitution (which is mainly unwritten but consists of understandings called conventions about how governments should behave), the document took shape.

The result: a peculiar but workable Constitution which provided for the establishment of a federal parliament, divided the powers to make laws between this new parliament and the states, had the Queen's representative at the head, and could only be changed by the majority of people in the majority of states.

There are those who argue that this foundation document should not be changed at all. They argue that the extraordinary social, economic and political developments of the 20th century require no response from governments and no evolving of structures or powers to deal with vastly different conditions, no change at all, they cry. Others say that the important issues of our time — political equality, the relationship of the individual to the state, human rights, the special consideration of the environment and international relations — demand specific attention in a Constitution.

An examination of the practical defects of the Constitution suggests that the former are an obstacle to proper reform. As for the arguments of the latter group, time will tell. It has been estimated that simple mechanical improvements to the Constitution, such as four-year parliamentary terms and simultaneous elections for the House of Representatives and the Senate would automatically save $80 million.

If we go one step further and suggest national protection standards instead of haphazard state-by-state standards, we can avoid incidents such as the "skimmer-box", a pool cleaning device that was banned in some states but caused injury to children in others where its use was allowed. And by introducing uniform consumer packaging laws, Australian households would save another $100 million every year.

It's ludicrous that in one nation we have two different union structures, three different railway gauges, more politicians per head than any other country in the world and now a burgeoning mail-order cigarette business in Queensland because of the inequality of state taxes.

In questions of family law, the Commonwealth has responsibility over the children from a marriage, but the States have responsibility for kids born outside a marriage. And so it goes on.

If one measurement of the health of a society is its ability to improve existing institutions, then it is probably time we got out of the sick bed and started thinking seriously about what changes can be made for the greater good.

It is said that the great obstacle in the way of changing the Constitution is the conservatism of the Australian people. I don't believe that. Rather, it has been the politicians who, through their conduct and language, have tended to politicise reform so that civilians are unable to make balanced assessments of the issues.

What a pity that Mr Howard has already signalled the Liberal Party's intention not to go ahead with the Constitutional Commission. On the one occasion that the whole community has been given the opportunity to participate in determining the structure of how Australia will work, the leader of one of the major parties in the country is playing the time-honoured "no change let's blame" routine that has characterised political dialogue since Federation and which accounts for the miserable spectacle made by the front page headlines of the newspapers that no one can be bothered reading any more.

By the way, it is estimated that the total cost of the Constitutional Commission will be $4 million — that's the same as the flagpole for the new Parliament House. Now that tells us something about the state of Oz politics, doesn't it ... Doesn't it?

Postscript

Reporting in July 1987 the Individual and Democratic Rights Committee proposed that, citizens initiative; one vote one value; protection of key legal procedures and core democratic freedoms; and recognition of Aboriginal Australians, be considered as possible changes to the Constitution.

ASSISTANCE TO
THE ARTS

In September 1986, Federal Parliament was presented with the results of an inquiry into Commonwealth Assistance to the Arts. One section of the 240 page report, *Patronage, Power and the Muse*, dealt with contemporary music. Among its findings was the recommendation that government-funded accommodation be provided for young Australian rock bands trying to make it in the major cities of the world.

It's a fickle business. It's a rat's life. It's show business!

Rock music: the end product of an industry that sells dreams through song, a business in which thousands set out for glory and only a handful make it. The rewards can be great if the success is international. Recognition, record sales and a career that spans continents: these are the goals of the many performers who leave home and head away to try their luck. Very few return.

The squats of Brixton and the swimming pools of Beverley Hills provide the backdrop which has been the gravestone of some of the finest bands this country has ever produced. The London tenement with sleeping bags on the floor, boards over the windows, another cup of tea and the memory of home's long hot summers has, more often than not, been the final resting place of young Australian musicians trying to "crack" the English music scene.

The Easybeats, the Masters Apprentices, Billy Thorpe & The Aztecs, Radio Birdman and the original Saints were amongst those who, having achieved a degree of notoriety in Oz, found the way blocked once they landed at Heathrow. *Bad management, bad timing, playing too loudly* and *talking too much* were all given as reasons for failure by the music press and public at home who expected great things from their rock heroes.

On the other side of the Atlantic, the scene was already "Corporate Rules, Ok!" Decisions about a band's future could be made in an instant by the side of a kidney-shaped swimming pool where (in various stages of intoxication, inebriation or undress) the casual and would-be hip record company executives analysed the likelihood of a band from "Austraaalia", wherever that is, becoming successful.

Daddy Cool, Skyhooks, The Dingoes and Cold Chisel, to name a few, foundered in a miasma of hype: "They're the new Beatles with funny accents" . . . artificial labels . . . "They're sort of heavy metal, punk, folk . . . you know," (voice trails off into the distance) . . . "Big business" . . . "How much money is there in it for us?" . . . plus there was the tendency for all

74

concerned to take credit when things were going well, but disappear when the going got tough.

Of course, no one ever pretended that making a mark on the world was that easy for Australian bands. But the simple fact was, and is, that the best of our local talent has always been as good as anything produced anywhere else in the world, if not better, and yet all have had a hard time trying to build careers in Europe and America.

Part of this is due to the tyranny of distance which is compounded by the associated costs involved with coming from a place a long way away. Then, there has been the natural reluctance on the part of England and America (both of which believe that the story of rock 'n' roll was, and is, written by them), to accept anything from a different place and give it a go.

What were the English to make of a burly guitar player called Billy Thorpe who screamed ''Suck more piss!'' at the top of his voice and played a fiery variety of boogie rock far louder than any band they'd ever heard at a time when gentility and acoustic music were making a brief resurgence . . . Or the American audiences of a band that dressed up in pelican costumes and said a good deal more than, ''Hi Phoenix, here's one for you!'' . . . Record and radio executives never quite came to terms with the strange pronunciation of the even stranger name of a band they couldn't categorise. Bad luck, Skyhooks.

In the Mother Country, Australian bands were long considered as beer-swilling, ex-colonial-Barry-McKenzie types better suited to swinging a cricket bat than a guitar. When playing in venues like the famous Marquee Club, where the likes of the Rolling Stones, Led Zeppelin, Queen, the Sex Pistols and The Clash and so on had been seen, the comparisons were inevitably bad.

For some, the only way out of this dilemma was to live and work there, so that eventually the English audience and press came to regard you as one of their own. AC/DC and the Birthday Party successfully travelled that route whilst making "good" music as they went. Unfortunately, many who followed have taken on the sound and look of a depressed and bitter Britain — black — and lost their own identity in the process. The result: Australian bands that sound like British bands. No thanks.

The big business of North America that dominates the rock industry makes it prohibitively expensive for a young band to build a career without the support of a record company that takes on the role of a large bank. A starting price of half a million dollars for albums, videos and associated promotion is a normal figure in today's pop music world.

With Australian dollar values and budgets, it's not surprising that, for local bands trying to crack it overseas, getting a record played on American radio is a critical factor in staying alive. But unless you're a big name artist, or you happen to produce a song that fits into the *Miami-Vice*-Contemporary-New-Wave-Funk format, or you have enough money to provide for some discreet bribery of radio station disc jockeys, then the chances of success are slim.

With the inevitable pressure from your financial backer (the record company), to provide a song which can be played on Radio WASP, the creative process undergoes a hammering and bands flounder; bland if they do and damned if they don't. The reason they started in the first place was to have some fun and the whole thing has suddenly become very serious.

Of course, there will always be some artists whose ability, dedication, talent and luck see them through the mire. Quality does tend to float to the top and real performers endure.

But why stop there?

Why not make records cheaper to produce and consume in our own country by removing the current sales tax of 22%? Why not subsidise local artists producing Australian music who are not in the mainstream and who do not have the backing of a big record company? In that way, diversity and depth in music would be encouraged, and of course, the spin-offs in terms of export income (once Australian records were properly promoted elsewhere) would be greater.

I am certain that bands would be prepared to repay the amount provided in direct assistance by the government if they happened to have world-wide success.

And it wouldn't be the end of the world if Dame Joan Sutherland and the Australian Opera took a cut in pay, would it? At least rock music is relevant to the times and, to a certain extent, characteristic of this country. The same cannot be said for some other art forms which are heavily supported by the taxpayers' money.

Finally, there's the question of where you want to live. For most performers the promise of free accommodation in the big cities of the world may induce them to travel away from their audience, their source of inspiration and their workplace in their attempt to make it overseas. But, in the end, I don't imagine many will ever be able to stay away for too long.

You see, there's something special about real Aussie bands and performers. They can still call Australia home.

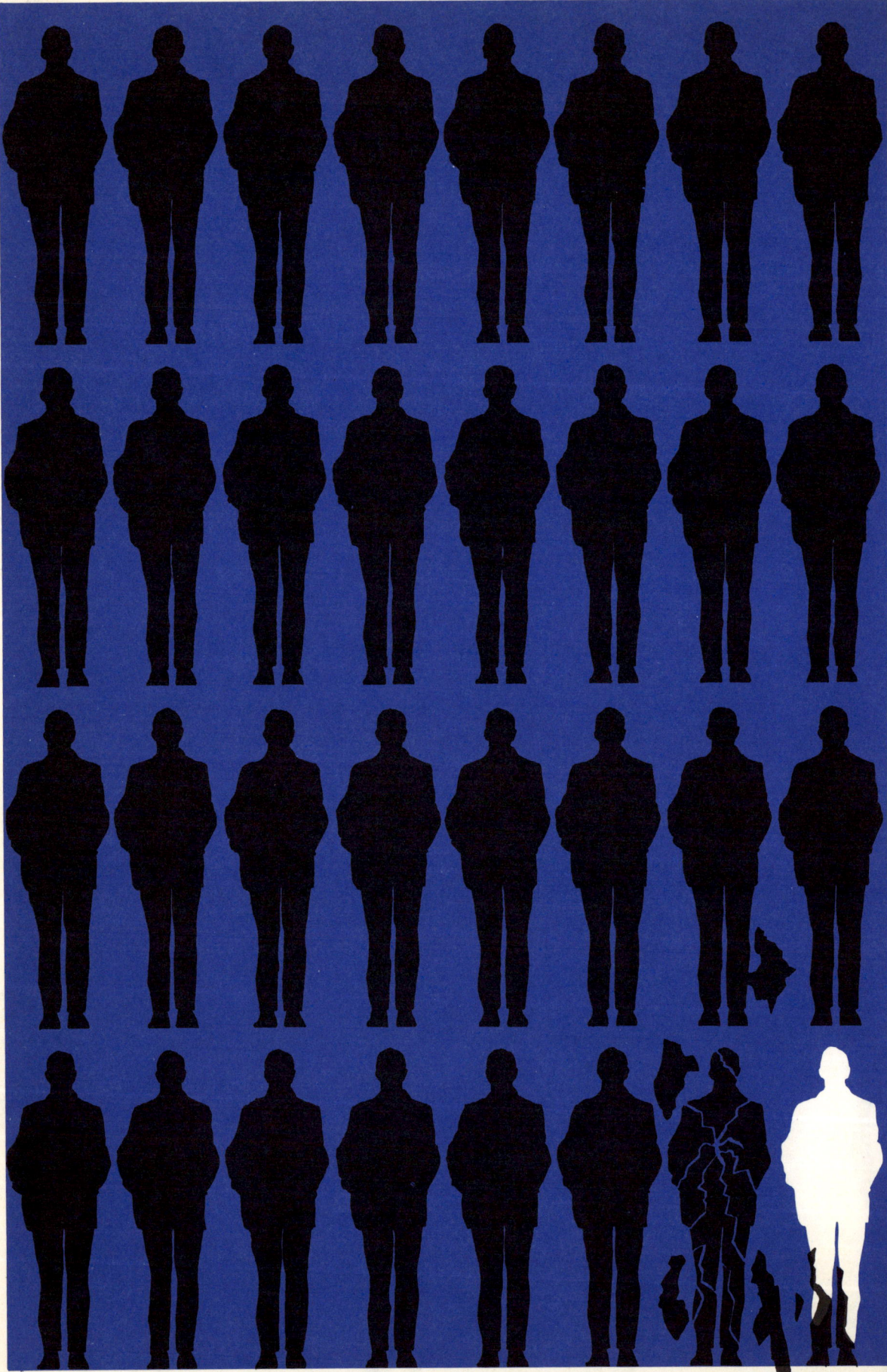

THE BEAT GOES ON

Judged the most boring so far, and called early despite repeated claims by the Prime Minister that parliament would run its full term, the 1987 election was a farce, notable only for the fact that the real issues — including foreign debt, unemployment, poverty, environmental degradation, the arms race, and the state of manufacturing and rural industries — were only rarely mentioned. Instead tax cuts was the main topic of debate with claim and counter claim, under the ceaseless media spotlight, the major aspect of the campaign. The Labor Party was returned to power with an increased majority.

We are standing in line singing "God Save The Queen". The asphalt is warming our feet, the cicadas are shouting us down. It is the Summer of '63 and the world is alive with new countries and lethal slingshots. Rolf Harris is a pop-star, Bob Menzies is boss and all is calm in the backblocks of White Australia.

We are learning Captain Cook's history, the Rum Corps, the squatter's ways and wheat. The map on the classroom wall shows us a country coloured Empire red. The great steam engine that is the Industrial Revolution is already running out of fuel. But that's all right. Atom power is here. "It's safe, it's clean, it's cheap, it's reliable," the scientists' chorus comforts us. We're saved.

Our world stretches as far as the Blue Mountains to the west, Manly to the east, from Sunday school to boy scouts, playing hide and seek round paling fences and into the bush where fantasy worlds begin in a cubby house made out of greengrocers' cases. Then the first television arrived in the street and we all became Texas rangers.

We grew up with the Beatles. Their music, their looks and a revolution that was signalled by long hair and loud music. Love songs turned into peace anthems and, one day in the middle of 1970, we leave school early, take the train into Martin Place and shout Vietnam away. Everybody wants to be in a band and the music from the southland begins to flow. Easybeats, Daddy Cool, Loved Ones, Max Merritt, Billy Thorpe, Axiom, Taman Shud — a host of noises, songs and fashions and great stuff it was too.

We danced in surf clubs and at the local hall, went to the sit-ins, checked out the new films, watched the street theatre and talked politics and drugs. Brian Henderson was Molly Meldrum in a suit. We were "stepping out", and the groups, all but ignored by local radio stations and record companies, headed for the great o/s. Most were ignored, fell apart and returned home to start again.

Sputniks and Apollos went up, with cameras turned on, and the world seemed so much smaller. Surfboards, hemlines and working hours got shorter; payrolls, flares and meter readings got longer. By now the average American home with air-conditioning, central heating, automatic kitchen appliances and two-car garage with automatic doors was burning as much energy in one week as a Third World village of one hundred people would use in a month. With space as the last frontier to be conquered and youth as the emerging social force anything seemed possible.

It was a time of excitement, a time to step into beyond. We elected a non-dinosaur government because "it was time".

It's November 1975 and we gather on the steps of the white dog-box. "Well may you say, 'God Save The Queen' because *nothing* will save the Governor-General," the voice of Whitlam booms across the crowd into the living rooms of suburbia. The brave new republic had foundered. We managed to quit someone else's war, get the vote and grew up a little in the process. But the global economy turned sour and so did the CIA when Pine Gap was scrutinized. Cabinet went to pieces. The rest is history. "Whatever Happened to the Revolution" became "All My Friends Are Getting Married" and the country went back to sleep again.

The ambitions of the Whitlam era — social and political reform, a more independent foreign policy, encouragement for the arts, provision of basic equitable treatment for the groups that were less well-off in society — these things are no longer part of the political agenda.

By 1987 the Labor government had become the natural conservative party in Australian politics. This is the time of broken promises, consensus and dark mutterings of a banana republic. The ideals of reform and social equity have been replaced by the dominant call for pragmatism. The country's millionaires are voting socialist. And on the other side of the fence the old conservative parties move even further across the ideological spectrum. New Right threatening to become Third Reich as spokespeople with cold eyes vow to bring Australia into a state of grace where the laws of the jungle prevail and "survival of the fittest" becomes the euphemism for treading the poor, the young, the minorities and those who don't believe in the cult of unfettered economic growth, as far down as possible.

The rationale behind the less-tax, less-government spending-leads-to-wealth-creation-and-a-better-place-to-live theory, is that in the end the riches will "trickle down" and end up in everybody's pocket. Rich people will buy more, there will be a greater demand for goods and services, thus stimulating employment and leading the economy into a boom.

So far there is little evidence that this has happened. In practice, the creation of wealth for a minority necessitates the majority being denied and things move back to the state of haves and have-nots. The economics of Apartheid is a clear example of this principle. Of course there is a need to rationalize economic production so as to provide for efficient *and* equitable distribution of goods and services. But vertical and horizontal integration, amalgamation and absorption of smaller economic units and adoption of technology to replace labour means that the boom period is inevitably short-lived. The free market never existed.

The global economy is dominated by the large corporations who have most of the capital and expertise. Thus relatively few economic structures determine the future of the whole. The multi-nationals' sorry record of support for Apartheid, continuing environmental neglect and political opportunism in the face of restrictions placed on their most profitable business — making bombs — does not engender any degree of confidence in the current preferred model of economic development.

It is no longer possible to consider the productive processes from whichever system they operate — be it the state-controlled capitalism of the Communist Blocs or Western transnational corporations — as wealth creating. They are in fact the opposite, for poverty is the natural state of the majority of the world's people, ecological devastation the logical conclusion of these activities so long as massive energy and resource use is a primary feature of economic activity. We *could* feed, clothe and educate every single person but this great richness of earth is being rapidly spent by the gargantuan beasts of commerce and industry. The major forms of modern economic activity which are required to sustain a highly materialistic lifestyle exploit humanity and nature to such an extent that the stage has been reached where the supposed benefits of the system are completely outweighed by the total costs to the global community, a price which must be tallied up at this moment and paid in years to come.

There is no such thing as a consumer-led recovery. The higher the standard of living, the greater the burden on future generations to repair the damage done by those "living it up" in the present.

Furthermore the majority of Third World countries, a good number of "developed" countries and several of the major world economies, most obviously the United States, are in debt. For many, this has come about as a direct result of arms purchases.

We live in a bankrupt, militarized, mixed-up, shook-up world.

If we look at earth as a bank and trace deposits and withdrawals since we crawled out of the cave, it has been a tale of heavy spending with few deposits. As hunter-gatherers we used up the surpluses provided by the natural eco-system. This income of bank earth was quickly spent once tools were put to use, so we drew on the capital of stored energy in trees to provide building materials and fuel. Farewell forests. Our income was then reduced but our ability to extricate hidden energy had grown. So we got stuck into our savings, the capital base of oil, coal and minerals, to rebuild our civilizations; and although this process is not of itself exhaustive and can tolerate repetition we have come to the point where our tools are so powerful that we can literally spend up the whole bank and will only be frustrated from doing so when the alarm bells start ringing loudly.

"Do not go into overdraft."
"Do not attempt to win that war."
"Why are the weather patterns so unpredictable?"
"What causes cancer?"
"*No* you can't always get what you want."
"There is no such thing as a free lunch."
"Crisis, what crisis?"

One way of looking at Gross National Product is to see it as a measurement of the processing of amounts of resources, within a certain period of time, into products which are consumed and/or discarded. So the production of the so-called luxuries of life turns the necessities, fresh air, clean water and fertile land, into rare commodities. The standard of living goes up but the quality of life plummets.

When I grew up people could not choose the sex of their offspring, the moon was a place spoken of in nursery rhymes and computers still took up most of the benchspace in the laboratory.

Now we are told that our big problems can still be solved by science's big technical solutions. The new magic word is biotechnology. Humans, prepare to go into overdrive, have faith, our machine will be able to make the world a better place. The industrial revolution, the dirty world is to be superseded by the world of information systems and life-altering processes. "It's safe, it's clean, it's cheap and it's reliable" — there's that chorus line of white coats and pocket calculators again.

In the past human inventions were applied to substances so as to derive supposed benefit for the whole species. Who can forget gunpowder and nuclear fission. Now we are reaching the stage where scientific invention, through the recombining of genetic matter, will be applied to other humans, as well as to plants and animals. It will be called the Golden Age of progress as laboratories design products from living things to fill up the post-industrial landscape.

The social, political and ecological consequences of such developments are so great that nuclear winter with its blanket horror will seem a lesser evil.

It is time to draw the line. To say quite clearly what we believe to be right and wrong and why we believe it. We may need to consider the Tao.

This is a collection of universal precepts which have made up the essential mores in all cultures and which by their nature are key components for a healthy society.

They are well known as inherent virtues, common admonitions for us to conduct our existence better.

"Treat your neighbour as you would yourself."
"Life is sacred and to be protected."
"Show compassion toward the less well off, the sick and the elderly."
"Respect your father and your mother,"
and so on.

In literate societies a study of ethics and the Bible was a part of the education of young people. In tribal societies, the rites of passage included specific instruction as to the laws of the culture, the prohibitions and the obligations. Thus "ought" replaced "must" when a context and a basis for human behaviour was established. Nowadays the form guide, instant lotteries and bucks nights have become a corral for those stuck between the perfect world of the advertisers and the strictures of family and the state.

For the most part the Judaeo–Christian ethic has guided the activities of the modern democracies; and yet rather than leading the world they seem intent on assisting its downfall.

This may be partly a result of misinterpreting the original instruction in Genesis for man to "be fruitful, and multiply and replenish the earth, and subdue it and have dominion over every living thing that moveth upon the earth". This has been taken to mean absolute domination of the planet. Surely this was not the intention of the author. We now know that one translation of subdue is "to act as viceroy", which means to be entrusted with the responsibility of looking after the king's domain, as his representative.

In the biblical context the God of Israel created both

earth and man, and saw that it was *good*; why then are we so determined to injure mother earth whilst seeking to further our own ends? In the process we wound ourselves. The two parts of the cosmos should not be separated. If they are, then we the species who possess language, tools and the freedom to choose our actions and have the ability to destroy and now to create, become God.

We have arrived at the beginning again; and yet at this black hole we catch a glimpse of what our world might become if we are to draw the line, accept our mortality and seek to infuse our being with a care for the existence of all other living things.

Earth's unique character, as the single garden planet, where life flourishes in diversity and abundance, imposes upon its most advanced species, humans, a complete responsibility for a stewardship imbued with knowledge of the ecological integrity of the whole and the shape that it must retain in order for life to go on.

For people to look ahead and away from the doom images of media, the war images of entertainment, the violence of political debate, the chaos of industrial life and the ominous threat of a final war, they must be able to believe in a different set of values.

Despite the repetition, banality and concurrence with the awful that much popular music displays, it is the ability of musicians to come together for a purpose other than pocket-filling which is an example of these values. BAND AID, ARTISTS AGAINST APARTHEID, the AMNESTY TOUR, STOP THE DROP, CONCERT FOR BANGLADESH — I could go on — show quite clearly that when musicians exercise their voice and give a moral focus the effect can be extraordinary. FEED THE WORLD didn't stop famine overnight but it went to the core of that part of the human spirit that is most honourable and offers hope in a dark time.

For some the very idea of a bunch of pop stars singing about starving people was too incongruous and affected to be valid. Such is the cynicism which pervades our society that beliefs are belittled and words like "compassion" and "love" are considered redundant outpourings of a romantic non-rational world.

I prefer to see this compassion as a springboard of the human conscience integral to our future survival — whether it comes from musicians or mechanics matters not — which will be an essential factor in the great struggle for a world where people can live with dignity, without fear, in an environment of peace and justice, safe in the understanding that the human endeavour has still got soul.

Let the beat go on.

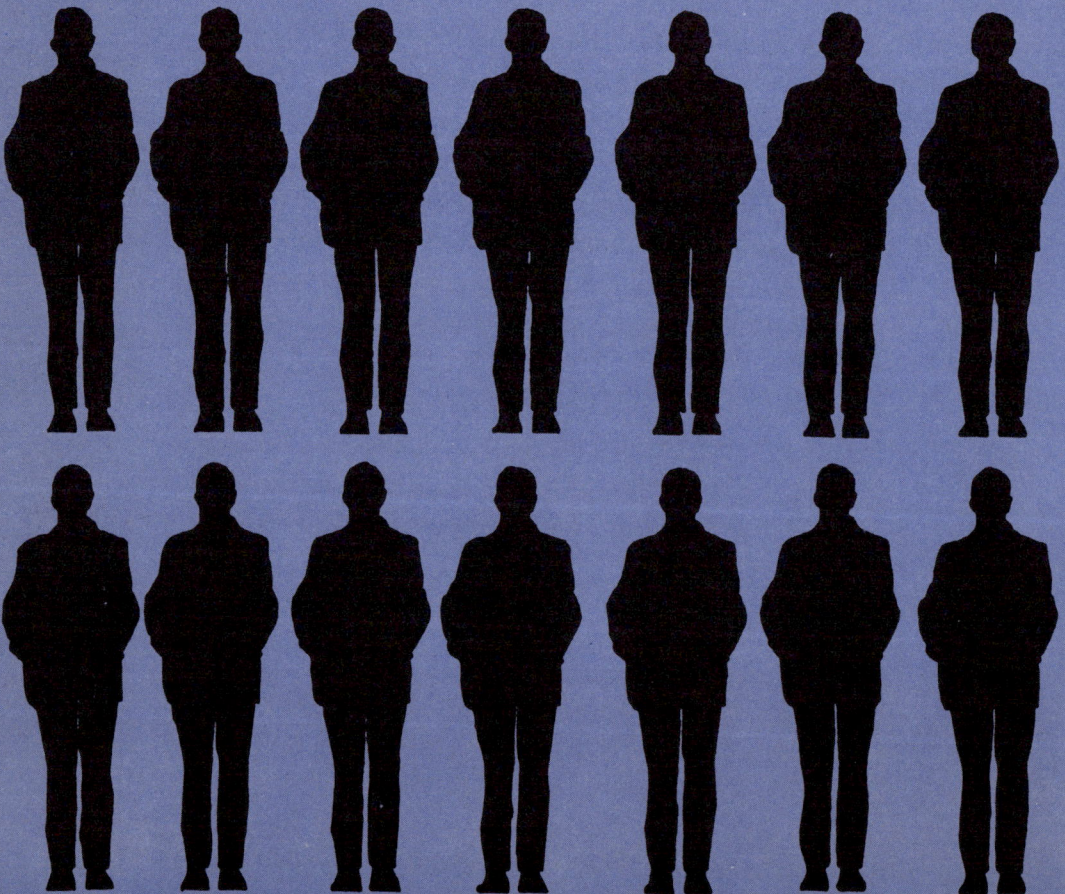

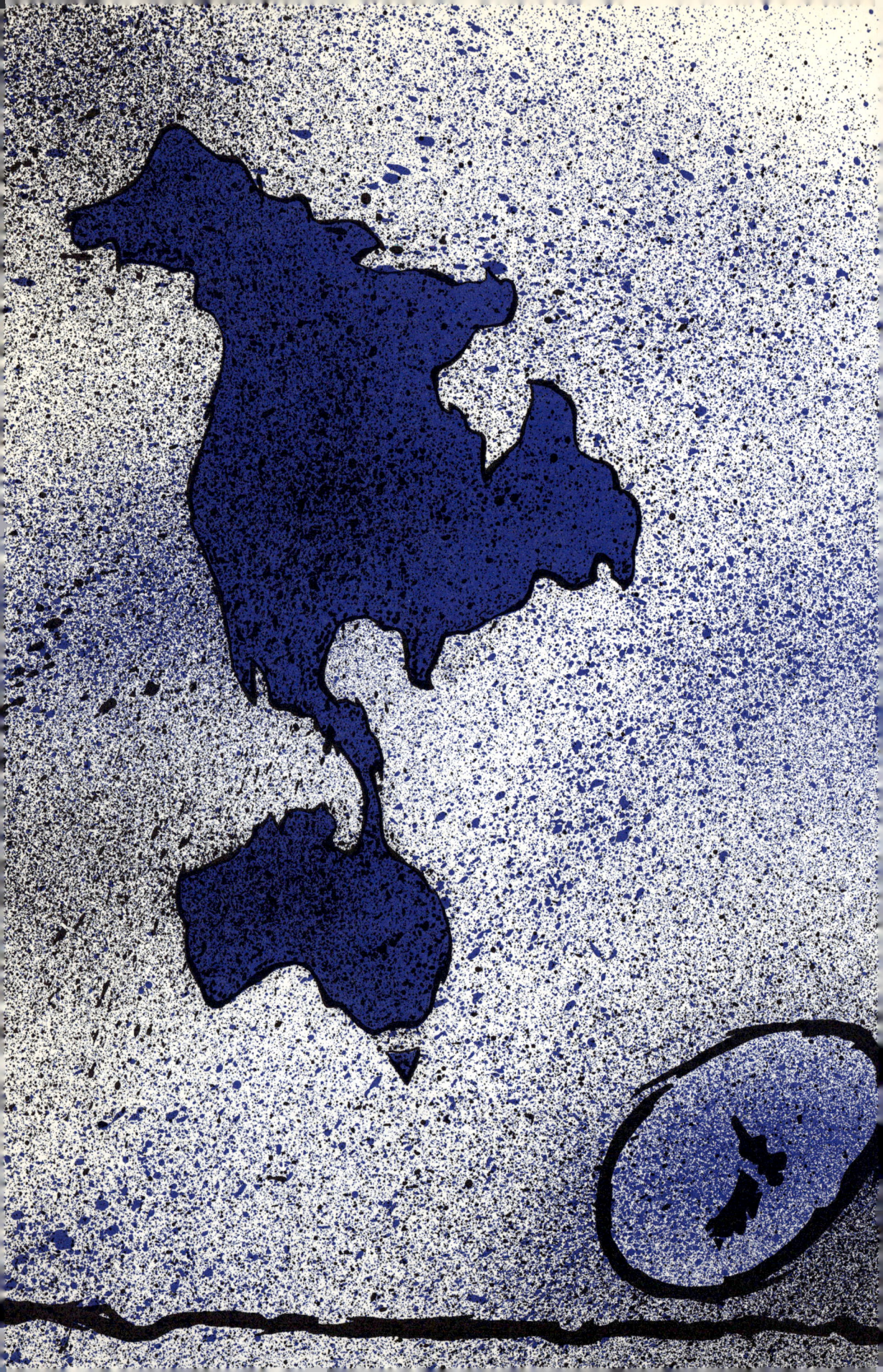

ANZUS

In late June 1986, the United States finally terminated its defence agreements with New Zealand because the elected government of the Shaky Isles refused to allow nuclear-armed ships into their harbours. But while the Kiwis were shown the door, Australia held firm to the weakened ANZUS alliance, despite the fact that the American spy bases at Pine Gap, Nurrungar and North West Cape are the biggest threat to our country's security.

I now pronounce thee master and slave.

Ever since Captain Cook and Co. first claimed this continent as British, conveniently ignoring the 40 000 years of settlement already in place, we've tended to shelter under the skirts of a great power who, we were led to believe, would protect us in times of peril.

Originally, it was the Mother Country, England. In 1899, our boys went off to her war against the Boers in what has since become the land of Apartheid. Later we went to her aid in World War I and World War II.

A few years ago I visited the National Portrait Gallery in London to look at a series of paintings and commentaries on World War I. Of course, I went to the Gallipoli pictures. But in the words underneath there was no mention of the role played by Australian and New Zealand soldiers. Nor was there any mention of the great casualties we suffered. So much for Britain's recognition of the glorious ANZAC tradition.

America's ascendancy during the turmoil of World War II saw us change skirts and cling to the all powerful GI denim. Thus the ANZUS tradition was born. We went out for them in Korea and Vietnam and today, through ANZUS (security treaty between Australia, New Zealand and the United States of America), we're joined together in defence co-operation in the Pacific region.

This week the "NZ" part of ANZUS left, so it's just us and President Reagan now, and we don't co-operate so much as do what we are told. Which generally means, "Shut up and behave like a skirt-holder, or else!"

The ANZUS treaty holds no guarantees. If anyone invaded Australia we could not be certain that the Americans would support us. The treaty only says that we will *talk* to one another if our "territorial integrity, political independence, or security" is threatened.

We'd talk on the telephone, I suppose, but I'm not sure what we'd say. For the irony of our close association with the US is that it is the very thing which threatens us the most. Who wants to be protected by a nuclear bomb?

Our defence experts agree that the Russians have neither the intention, nor the capability, to attack Australia. And yet, the major risk to this country is the threat of nuclear war. The reason that that threat exists is because we have the so-called "joint" (but in real life, "American") military communications bases dotted around our country.

This collection of white balls, aerials, computer rooms and no-go-for-Aussies areas is part of the complex design-for-use system of military linkages that the United States maintains on Australian soil. Because they're on our soil, we have Soviet nuclear weapons pointed in our direction.

If Mr Reagan should decide to do battle with the Soviets, then the price of ANZUS (without "NZ") would indeed be high.

We are told that by allowing the US facilities to sit on our land, we are contributing to the maintenance of the state known as "deterrence". (A fair definition of "deterrence" would be two lunatics standing in a 44 gallon drum of petrol. In one hand is a gushing petrol pump; in the other, an open box of matches. The lunatics are shouting abuse at each other and digging for oil at the same time.)

By having the US bases here, we're told we're keeping the world safe as well as putting pressure on the Americans for disarmament. But the Americans are turning the Pacific into a nuclear lake. Urged on by a Clint Eastwood type named Lehman, who believes in winning wars, the US has built the most powerful fleet of warships that our world has ever seen. They test their weapons in the Pacific, including new arrivals such as Tomahawk (a small and accurate nuclear Cruise missile of the sea) which are not even included in the counting when the two sides sit down for the regular Geneva talk-fest. In a revision of the ANZUS Treaty in 1970, the Americans said they would protect us with their "nuclear shield", (gulp), otherwise "We shall look to the nation directly threatened to assume the primary responsibility of providing manpower for its defence".

Known as the "Nixon Doctrine" it was implemented by the US President who cheated, swore, broke the law, got caught and finally resigned on the eve of his impeachment. (The ex-president is now on the come-back trail as an author and an expert on foreign affairs. But that's showbiz — sorry, politics.)

The point of all this is to draw attention to three important things which happened recently.

Firstly, the Dibbs Report on Australia's future defence strategy was released. Echoing the Nixon Doctrine, it said that we have to stand on our own two feet. But whilst Mr Dibbs won't admit it, in so doing, his report acknow-ledges that ANZUS is on the way out.

Secondly, New Zealand left the ANZUS fold. Peeved that the Kiwis don't want US nuclear war ships in their ports, the Americans didn't even want to discuss the divorce. *Aoteoroa* has now become a small but significant force in the struggle for a real nuclear free Pacific.

Thirdly, in a series of non-violent demonstrations in New South Wales and South Australia, local people continued to express their view of the ANZUS tradition. At Nurrungar near Adelaide, the US commander of the satellite reconnaissance base was presented with an eviction order and asked to leave. Obviously South Australians don't like the idea of Reagan's Star Wars proposal any more than the US Union of Concerned Scientists does.

I look forward to the day when the eviction notices are formally presented to the American Secretary of State by the elected leader of the Australian people.

Come on, Aussie, come on.

HAPPY BIRTHDAY

 40

 80

 120

 160

 200

 **AUSTRALIA**

BICENTENARY

In January 1988 the bread & circuses
bureaus of our major advertising
agencies and government departments
are set to launch a barrage of jingoistic
jingles boasting of this country's
achievements since the arrival of the
British colonists 200 years ago. But
behind this façade of corporate-
sponsored back-slapping lurks the
fundamental question that is likely to be
buried beneath the waves of celebratory
hysteria: Where do we go from here? Do
we construct a vision for the future of
this nation? Or we do continue to set
the wrong priorities and continue the
down-hill slide?

Will the birthday noises of 1988 sound like a celebration or a funeral?

In the commemoration of our short 200 year spell, will we have cause to be proud? Or will we be so racked by division and turmoil that the sounds of cash registers ringing will be drowned by the collective moan of those who've been let down by their leaders, by those who will be forced, for the rest of their lives, to carry the neglect that quick-fix politics have included?

If the Prime Minister is serious about his address to the nation, then he'll tell us that the decline of Western civilisation has arrived and is knocking hard on the doors of Parliament House.

The *decline* I write of is agreed on by many, but few can find assent to the common causes. One thing is certain, and that is that the *decline* or *crisis*, call it what you will, is reaching a critical stage and it's you and I who will have to confront it.

An example of the crisis is the growing gap between the rich and the poor of Australia.

One would hope that with its abundant resources and healthy, educated population this would not be a feature of our so-called egalitarian society.

Yet the Australian Council of Social Services estimates that nearly two million people are living below the poverty line. This disgracefully high figure exists at a time when the wealthy are becoming even wealthier and stock exchange profits are at a record high.

Meanwhile, as youth unemployment continues to rise, CEP schemes are being cut back and the national debt (the amount we owe the rest of the world) is going into double figures at the billion level. If INXS hadn't managed a Top Ten hit in the US that figure would be even higher.

In the face of this dilemma, our greatest priority is the development of real long term programs which address the question of work, and what form it should take for future Australians. How it's to be created and how it's to be paid for, and what it should entail.

But because of their concern with short term power rather than long term policies, neither political party is capable of coming to terms with that particular issue.

They see the development of industry as the answer. But this is 1986, not '56. The *post*-industrial age is upon us. If you want to produce motor cars or modems for the consumer world, then you have to do it more efficiently than anyone else. And that means better quality and lower prices. Technology can assist, but normally it means machines doing the job, not people.

The promise of a better world through progress via technology has become a lie. The space shuttle Challenger will fly again, but only because the American dream demands it, not because it will feed or clothe people who live in cardboard boxes in the avenues of New York.

Don't expect high-tech to provide the solution either.

Artificial babies with a survival chance of one in ten, along with extremely serious questions about the ethics of gene engineering is the best we can do. The scientists and the corporations have neither learned the lessons of Einstein nor remembered his principles of thermodynamics.

These laws of nature may be unchangeable, but they are not depressing nor should they be considered the reason for our decline. Failure to observe the laws may justly be considered as one of the causes, but we are the matters of our own destiny, are we not?

Just because our leaders think like dinosaurs, doesn't mean we have to act like *T. Rex*.

We owe our wealth to the sheep's back and what we've dug out of the ground, but our future wealth will be determined by what values we adopt as central principles in our development as a nation, by the foresight and will of those who govern us indicating that their politics take the future into account, whilst appreciating the qualities of the past.

Leaders like Mr Hawke who play golf with Foreign Secretaries of countries which seem to believe that the meaning of life can be gleaned from episodes of *Magnum PI* aren't much help.

Neither are leaders like Queensland Premier Sir Joh Bjelke-Petersen who with the support of only 30% of the electorate take delight in knocking down every historic building or razing every bit of wilderness that gets in the way of their own ideas of development. Or leaders like former New South Wales Premier Neville Wran who resigned before going to the polls with a legacy of monument building, plans for the biggest casino in the southern hemisphere, a toy town monorail, and a giant hotel complex. All this in the biggest urban centre in the land, in a congested city in which thousands of kids have nowhere to sleep at night and where all are crying out for a bit of open-space instead of cracked concrete and cracked smiles.

Leaders for whom pre-election promises mean little more than a test of the gullibility of their constituency, for whom the power and the prestige of office is the greatest goal and damn the consequences: we can all behave like hooligans at a witch hunt, scream abuse at each other whilst trashing the country and then pick up parliamentary privileges and a fat pension when our time is up. The only dance they seem to know is the one which goes "show me how high to kick up my legs oh beloved

leader of a country bigger than ours from a long way away".

I'm proud to be an Aussie boy, but it sickens me to the heart that we grovel in Washington, let them use us as they please, and then can't even get them to buy our beef. It makes you almost nostalgic for the glory days of the big men, Fraser and Whitlam. Well, almost.

Former Prime Ministers Curtin and Chifley showed us that we can produce leaders with a sense of vision, not sheep who follow the blind instinct of the herd, fed on fear and the junk culture which is collapsing around our ears at this very moment.

Boom–Crash . . . Welcome, 1988.

THE NEW RIGHT

Out of the industrial disputes at Mudginberri in the NT and Robe River in WA the so-called New Right sprang to national prominence in 1986. It was seen by some as a newspaper beat-up that got out of hand, whipping up such a storm that the alleged proponents of the movement had no choice but to join in. The result was the germination of divisive ideas that are likely to affect our nation's social and political system for some time to come.

The Chinese philosopher Lao Tsu thought that life could be seen and explained in terms of a circle. Nothing was new, but nothing stayed the same. You always ended up in the same place, although you could be further ahead than when you started.

Sounds familiar doesn't it? Like the authors of astrology guides in the daily newspapers, Lao wasn't taking any chances. But he had a point.

The selling of Coca-Cola and the ideas of the New Right share a similar quality. Neither contains anything new. The promotional campaigns both say the same thing over and over again and once you've absorbed them you're in the same position as you were before you knew about them.

The campaign to sell Coke and the New Right are bound up by the same strands of high-finance-induced myth creation, cemented by repetition.

Of course, Coke pays for its advertisements. And it's palatable. You can get it down on a hot day, so it does the job, not of making you a happy member of the "now" generation dancing with attractive smiling people in the litter-free fun-filled beach — but it does quench your thirst.

The New Right, on the other hand, doesn't need to pay for its advertisements. Sympathetic media takes care of that problem with regular dollops of free publicity. But the message dressed up to attract us with the simple slogan of "The unions have too much power" is a smoke screen behind which lurks a philosophy that is both difficult to swallow and certain to cause this country a good deal of harm, should it be taken seriously.

The concept of the New Right is the politics of money and power. It's the ideology of greed, filled by an unbridled commitment to individualism. It leaves no

room for social equity, compassion or the idea of an egalitarian society.

That uniquely Australian quality of "We're-in-this-together-and-no-one-should-be-considered-to-be-anything-other-than-equal" that's been an integral part of politics in this country since the first European settlement is one that is rejected by the proponents of the New Right.

The New Right is made up of leading business executives, employer organisations, some farmers' organisations, a few conservative academics, and anybody else who hasn't witnessed the divide and fall of Thatcher's Britain.

Like Mr Reagan, Mrs Thatcher is very New Right. Most New Right leaders are, in fact, old. The idea of the New Right itself is very old as well. It's as old as slavery from whence it derives its inspiration and to which, in the form of South Africa, it continues to pay homage.

The New Right believes that neither government nor associations of working people (unions), should be able to restrict the proper application of capital (money) in the economy. People, in their view, either sink or swim. And if they sink, well that's too bad. Because according to the New Right, welfare is not good for business.

The New Right, it seems, often meets in secret. They are pro America, pro nuclear weapons, pro the monarchy, pro big business and pro development. They are anti conservation, anti union, anti peace movement, anti multiculturalism and anti government. Mr Howard, leader of the Liberal Party, agrees with their views. Sir Joh Bjelke-Petersen has their support.

One New Right vision for a future Australia depicts a scene with mini-nations instead of states; a continent without a federal parliament, without social welfare, public health or education, without any co-ordination of

trade or economic policies. It's an absurd viewpoint which goes some way towards explaining why New Right business is having such a hard time. Is a revolution — in which business has the right to get whatever it wants — in the best interests of the working people of this country? I don't believe it is. Neither, thankfully, does Mr Hawke.

I'm a member of a union, but I've never been put in a position where I've had to go out on strike. And although I'm sometimes frustrated when the union does its job badly, I support without reservation the right of all working people to join together so as to preserve and protect their livelihoods.

Of course, unions need to be more sensitive to the realities of modern economic conditions. Sectarian attitudes and greed serve the cause of labour badly. But the fact is that Australia's strike record has been improving in recent years and has now fallen to the approximate figure of two hours per worker per year that's lost due to industrial activity.

Still, we are in critical times and Australia requires a reassessment of the relationship between labour and capital, a reassessment which takes into account the politics of industrial democracy, profit and job sharing, and long term planning which allows for the proper protection and preservation of our environment. What we don't need is the "kick-the-worker-today-and-take-the-money-tomorrow" attitude that comes from the Cold War warriors who are currently at work around the place.

The only way in which the country can work properly is for management and labour to co-operate with one another, not condemn one another.

But the sad truth is that condemnation is the only language that the New Right appears to understand. Take

this quote from New Right leader, Peko-Wallsend boss
Charles Copeman,

> It isn't a matter for conciliation, it's a matter
> for arbitration. We are not prepared to
> conciliate!

Obviously the inevitable expansion of capital with its
attendant social inequality and natural destruction brooks
no interference and allows for no moral judgements.

What a great pity that the glorious mess of money
and guns that makes up part of the world we see on
television every night is the vision of the New Right come
true. Mr Howard and his colleagues should not be
encouraged to allow it to come any closer to home.

LAND RIGHTS

In August 1986, a federal government
caucus committee met to amend the
Commonwealth's Land Rights Law (NT).
It was a move that was resisted by
Aboriginal representatives from the
Northern Lands Council and Central
Lands Council on the ground that the
proposed changes ignored the views of
Aboriginal people and left little room for
negotiation. The proposed changes
would have removed rights achieved for
Aboriginal people under a Liberal
government and thwarted progress
towards self-determination.

*"It is you who have devoured the vineyard,
the spoil of the poor is in your houses. What
do you mean by crushing my people, by
grinding the face of the poor?"*

Isaiah 3:14–15

Riots on the steps of the ''Taj Hawke'' dominate news headlines in '88 . . . the Bicentenary boycott . . . Aborigines and the unemployed withdraw . . . United Nations representatives visit Australia to decide whether we should be included in the South African sanctions . . . mining companies bankroll the formation of a new political party . . . Lang Hancock is the proposed leader.

How poor is poor? Well according to an old *Guinness Book of Records*, the poorest people in the world live in the western desert of Central Australia . . . out there in the deserts of the Northern Territory and Western Australia where the land is big and red and the climate harsh.

Australia's deserts do not have many Hollywood sand-dunes. (In fact a French film crew who came here to shoot desert scenery had to import their own sand — and that was for a nature documentary!) In Australia's deserts it is windy a lot of the time. It's very hot in summer, very cold in winter . . . the Equator to the Antarctic all wrapped up in one gigantic environment. It's a beautiful, bold, ageless country. This is the heartland of Australia.

In the past, Aborigines suffered the indignity of having their land taken from them, or being corralled into special settlements and reserves. They developed record rates of infant mortality, unemployment, imprisonment of young people, and numerous other malaises of the modern age.

The cultures had clashed and European civilisation had left its mark.

Faced with the possibility of extinction and armed only with a desire to see justice done by being able to return to the lands where their forefathers had lived for centuries, Aborigines embarked on a campaign for genuine home ownership. It's called land rights. But in

110

this case the home they wanted to live in was one they had never sold.

Limited recognition to this important fact was given in the late 1960s in a report handed down by a judge named Woodward. As a result, a Northern Territory Land Rights Act was introduced. It allowed traditional owners of Aboriginal land to go back and claim their homelands provided that the land they wanted to live on was either Crown land or land that nobody else owned.

Both major political parties supported this activity. In fact, the entire population decided by referendum in 1967 that Aboriginal people should be counted as Australians, and that the Commonwealth should have responsibility for them. We were really making progress.

Amongst those desert people who've been described as the poorest in the world are a tribal group called the Pintupi. They finally left Papunya — the government settlement into which they'd been trucked in the late fifties — and returned to their traditional tribal country 500 kilometres west of Alice Springs five years ago. Now they're building a new community called Kintore on a windswept stretch of desert near the Western Australian border.

They have their own council which employs teachers and mechanics and oversees the day-to-day business of the community.

But conditions are rough. It's dry and windy country. The people live in cement huts or humpies made of corrugated iron and canvas. Getting to the nearest hospital entails a six hour drive over bumpy dirt roads.

The Pintupi people have "strict rules". Alcohol is completely banned in the community. Petrol sniffing, which has reached the epidemic stage in some settlements, has been controlled. The local arts & crafts collective is turning in a reasonable profit. The school is being improved, shower blocks built, water supplies extended and football fields laid.

All this by a people who, as recently as fifteen years ago, were being rounded up by officers of the now-defunct Native Affairs Branch and sent into Papunya on another tribe's land, where they were given khaki uniforms and three Whitefella meals a day. Unaccustomed to European eating habits, and forced to live in foreign country, many of them died. (Of the 72 Pintupi people rounded up and chucked into Papunya between 1963 and August 1964, for instance, 35 died within a few months.)

The essential element in the renaissance of the Pintupi people has been their decision — against the wishes of government bodies — to return to their traditional tribal country.

From their example, it is obvious that the minimum necessity for the continuation of the Aboriginal race as a whole is to gain access to, and control of, their own lands.

And yet this week, under the guise of better administration of the resources that lie in the land for all Australians, we see the federal cabinet considering a proposal to reduce the rights that Aboriginal people have fought so strongly for.

The argument presented is that Aboriginal people have too much power in their right of veto over the exploits of mining companies on their land. But this argument denies the fact that, under current legislation, the federal government retains the power to override any veto that may be exercised by Aboriginal people. It also denies that, under the same legislation, it cannot be fairly said that such developments have been hindered.

The great myth of the veto has always been a smoke screen designed to allow unfettered access by the mining company wolf pack — many of whom remit their profits to their overseas head offices direct from quarry Australia. In this light, I'd like to quote directly from a letter signed by Mr Holding, the Minister for Aboriginal Affairs, on 6 August 1986 in which he says . . .

> The mining industry has sought to make out that the veto or the threat of it has been largely responsible for holding back mineral exploration and development in the Northern Territory. I agree with you that this is not the case.

In this letter — addressed to the adviser of the Catholic bishops in Australia — Mr Holding offers to listen sympathetically to any proposals that the Catholic bishops may have. I wonder why he's not listening to the Aboriginal people who've been unanimous in their rejection of the proposed changes to land rights legislation.

These changes include allowing greater power to the Minister in relation to determining issues of development, and providing the Northern Territory government with special rights in relation to Aboriginal land, and, worst of all, reducing the amount of, and categories of, land which can be claimed by Aborigines.

The effect of this will be to completely undermine the principles of inalienability — that is, the ''cannot-be-tampered-with-ness'' of the legal title — and compensation for use of Aboriginal land: the one thing they need to ensure their future!

I think I know where the Catholic bishops will stand on this matter, but in consideration of the Bicentenary let's go one stage further in the morality stakes and suggest to Mr Hawke that the ancient law of Israel known as the Jubilee be introduced as a principle of government by consensus.

Under the law of the Jubilee, every fifty years all land was returned to the original owners, all debts were forgiven, and all slaves freed, thereby returning things to an equal state. Since the wealthy tended to become more so, this was seen as a proper and necessary way of promoting an equitable society.

It sounds like the sort of ideal that the Labor Party used to uphold.

QUEENSLAND

In Queensland the pervading attitude amongst the governing politicians appears to follow the thinking that bigger-is-better. It's an idea that also appears to have taken root amongst our scientists. The long-term repercussions of such an approach, however, are likely to be detrimental.

It's a big big country but it's a small small world.

John Kennedy's "Love Gone Wrong"

Thank God, Russ Hinze is not a scientist, or the Queensland of the future would probably look like the abandoned movie set of *Boys' Own State*, an epic real-life story of hi-tech innovation and imagination with one giant bullock on the Darling Downs, ten office-block-size sugar cane plants sitting between Townsville and Cairns, and an enormous five thousand square kilometre gaol somewhere south of Mt Isa for all those people who still wanted to vote in elections.

Australia's Texas in the Deep North has, in a number of ways, always embraced the notion that "Size is Superior". Take, for example, the profusion of giant objects which mark different tourist locations around the state. Often models of fruit or animals, they include the giant pineapple, the giant mango, the big cow and, my favourite, the giant lawnmower.

Between the Gold Coast (home of the beaches with the longest high-rise shadows in the Western World) and Brisbane, there are numerous fun parks and amusement complexes each claiming to be the Biggest Giant Water Slide in The Southern Hemisphere, huge shopping plazas and massive subdivisions with instant suburbs all named "Glorious Estates". Such developments are made possible by the giant bulldozer which is often driven by the Minister for Main Roads, the giant Mr Hinze who was recently defeated in the Biggest Beer Belly in the World competition by Queensland's fattest truck driver.

Then there's the Premier, Sir Joh Bjelke-Petersen. The longest serving state leader with one of the largest gerrymanders in the country, he's the Minister of the Police Department with the greatest powers, recipient of the largest defamation settlement and originator of the greatest amount of hyperbole heard in years. The Libyan-Terrorists-in-Nunawading is the most recent example.

118

In a state where the government and the police have the greatest power and people, as a result, have the least, Queensland law provides that it can be deemed illegal for three or more to gather together for a conversation. Do not protest, do not appeal to the court, go directly to gaol ...

When it comes to development, Queensland has always said "Yes! And make it big!" Surfers Paradise is the best-known example of the we-are-building-a-better-state ethos. There, where the suicide rate for the over-60s is the highest in Australia, southern pensioners with money and skin to burn closet themselves in the concrete of jerry-built high rise towers that throw shadows across the beaches by three in the afternoon.

Queensland, where government is big business and growth is the magic word, where development is the way forward and the unemployment rate is the highest in the land.

Queensland, where development needn't be hindered by tiresome regulations, environmental impact statements and unions.

At the same time as the Deep North believes it can build its way out of trouble, scientists are suggesting that there might be another way. As a way to progress via productivity, the biology age is introducing the development of entirely new species of plants and animals.

After the splitting of the atom came the splitting of DNA, the building block of life. It was a breakthrough that gave scientists the ability to go past mating blocks and species borders to produce new combinations of living things. By experimenting with genes, scientists have become the architects of life. The so-called super-pig is amongst their most recent inventions. The scientists justify

119

their work by describing a tantalising picture of super-crops and giant animals to feed the world's starving, and new super drugs to cure the world's diseases. Science will conquer all.

Such myopia disguises a central truth of the natural world: the laws of entropy require that matter created will see a correlated diminishing of energy, and that there is a limit and balance in the planet's ecosystem.

Never mind the side issues of the already existing mountains of food that are stored around the Western World; the reality of society-induced illness, the fact that over half of the world's scientists earn their living by dreaming up better ways to kill people ... the bottom line is the finiteness of our planet.

This talk of a future in which biotechnology creates living things that will make our lives better ignores the absolute reality that these things (whether super-crops or super-animals) require life-supporting systems to keep them alive and that it will never be possible to create an ecosystem in the laboratory which will feed the genetically improved corn cob.

It may be ten times larger, disease resistant and exotic yellow with a built in "bar-b-que" flavour, but it will also require ten times more nourishment to make it grow. In a world where soil erosion and depletion is a major concern, the last thing we need is giant vegetables sucking every last nutrient out of the earth at the rate of knots.

The fact that the new organisms are unpredictable, uncontainable and can reproduce at will should tell us that such developments will bring the most extreme consequences. Yet this week the CSIRO told us they were building a special "safe" (their word) laboratory to allow genetic experiments on various plant strains.

Our scientists obviously haven't learned the lessons of the recent past. A couple of years ago, General Electric developed the Micus organism which was designed to eat oil spills. But it was never released because of the fear that it may well have multiplied and ended up in the engines of every motor car in the world.

Multiply the number of potential organisms by the biggest figure you can think of and you'll get some idea of the scale of the problem.

Nature does not provide a free lunch. Is it to be Daintree Rainforest or development? The Queensland Minister for the Environment allowed the destruction of an area of rainforest from which a substantial number of the world's known plant species have come. It was joined to one of the greatest natural wonders in the world, the exquisitely fragile Great Barrier Reef. Amazingly, Australian scientists stayed silent over this act of ecological vandalism that will affect generations of earth dwellers for millenia to come.

What we take, we must pay for. There is a cost for all developments. The disappearance of the planet Earth behind the thumbs of an astronaut 20 000 miles into space tells us that we have our place in the universe and that that place is to look after and care for our common home.

May the year of the super-pig be the year when Queensland returns to its common home.

IN VITRO FERTILISATION

Australia leads the world in In Vitro Fertilisation (Fertilisation Under Glass). A method of fertilising a female egg outside the human body and then implanting the egg in the mother. It was first successfully used in Lancashire, UK, in July 1978. Since then, Australian scientists working out of Monash University have developed the process and now lead the world in the field. It is a science that is likely to have some astounding repercussions on the future of mankind.

There's a new supermarket in town selling the ultimate product: a created being. And the only things you need to walk through the automatic checkout with a real person under your arm are lots of money, the inclination to play guinea pig and a belief in one of the creeds of the age of enlightenment, that science can overcome what nature has denied.

We are ready to let the Edelstens of the world play God (the concept Edelsten is based on the Sydney doctor of the same name who ran 24 hour glam rock medical clinics, owned an Australian football club and generally made a lot of hot moves around town). For a price, you can sing like Diana Ross. BYO sequinned jumpsuit and you can even look like her too. Sensational! And once your career is launched you can pay off the mortgage you owe to the sperm bank and you're a free clone.

Einstein, the great scientist of soul, once remarked that "God does not play dice". And yet Australia leads the world in the development of a new technology that sees man (for it is mainly males who are involved in all this) engaging in a determined and ultimately frightening process of doing just that. In the name of progress, the pursuit of human happiness and free enterprise, the process is carried out with a view to profit and has a greater margin than two-up.

Doctors can create babies without the sperm of the father (and here I mean husband or partner) fertilising the egg of the mother inside her womb.

This process we know as In Vitro Fertilisation (IVF). We've all seen the happy couples on the news and in the *Women's Weekly*. Where previously they were infertile, they now have an instant family. Four or five little test tube babies are held up by the proud parents, the TV lights flash and the doctors gaze upon it all in their beneficent wisdom.

Providing babies for parents who cannot naturally conceive a child is understandably a wonderful thing. But such instant happiness carries a cost and calls into question the role of science in honeymoons, the meaning of life, and the future shape of the human race. Deep water . . . and we're in it up to our necks.

In the process of creating a test-tube baby it is normal practice for doctors to fertilise a number of female eggs, thereby manufacturing spare embryos which sit in the fridge. Science has an inordinate drive to experiment with the embryos, just as it wishes to fulfil the desires, however reasonable, of those who seek to make use of the "make-a-baby" technologies.

What are we to make of a future where a man can become pregnant, where all children are sterilised at birth after a sample of eggs and sperm have been taken, where someone conceived in 1986 is born in 2086? These possibilities which have already been publicly canvassed by scientists, are endless: choosing sex, twinning, cloning, producing disease-free hybrids . . . Mind bending, isn't it?

Who controls these reproduction technologies and to what ends? What are the rights of biological mums, the breeders in a rent-a-womb situation? What rights does the embryo have? When does research end and eugenics (the philosophy Nazi Germany adopted to justify killing millions of Jewish people) begin?

Our government clearly has decided on its priorities. The National Health and Medical Research Council has endorsed the national technology strategy. In 1985 breast cancer research received $270 000 whilst medicine and technology got $1.8 million.

A test-tube baby can cost Mum and Dad up to $10 000 and the success rate is varied. Around 20% seems to be an average figure. The cost to the rest of us has been estimated at around $20 000 per baby. Our own highly publicised Monash University team has now set up a business in the US where nearly half the baby clinics have never sent a patient home with a baby. One report shows 600 women treated, $2.5 million paid over in fees, but not one single infant delivered.

The perfect life will be made into an absolute ideal when we fool ourselves into thinking we can create a better species to inhabit our world. What characteristics should that species have? Tall with blonde hair? Who decides? And what are the criteria for making these decisions? Intelligence? Size of biceps? Lack of criminal record in parents? Ability to understand the plot line of *Crocodile Dundee*?

How much will parents be charged to be provided with a baby boy with a strong right foot? How much will the boy be charged — when he grows up and plays for one of Dr Edelsten's football teams — to find out who his real mother was?

The thought of controlling evolution will be irresistible to megalomaniacs, paranoiacs and social engineers. In other words, politicians.

Imagine the scenario. Federal cabinet meets in Canberra on a chilly winter's morning. The trade figures look worse than ever. Despite the Kakadu deposits, the price of uranium is the lowest it has ever been. Despair is in the air.

The enigmatic Senator John Button, Minister for Industry, disturbs the silence with a thought, "Listen, Prime Minister. We'll marry the worst of your big chat to the nation with the worst of my ideas about how to make Australian industry competitive.

"We'll breed dozens of Deeks and Joans, Bens and . . . whoever the others were, for every suburb in every

126

state. We'll order 5000 finished embryos from Monash University Creating Children Corporation Pty Ltd, after all, the taxpayers helped get them off the ground. We'll check each infant for moustache and lung size, give Alan Bond the franchise to service the community, throw in a reasonable commission but restrict sponsorship until they're over six months old, and there we have it — *Terra Australis*, the greatest sporting nation in the world. We'll breed a race of supermen!''

I can feel a baby boom coming on . . .

Postscript

In March 1987 the Vatican instructed Roman Catholics throughout the world not to engage in In Vitro Fertilisation. The Vatican forbade what it described as the treatment of human beings as objects of experimentation.

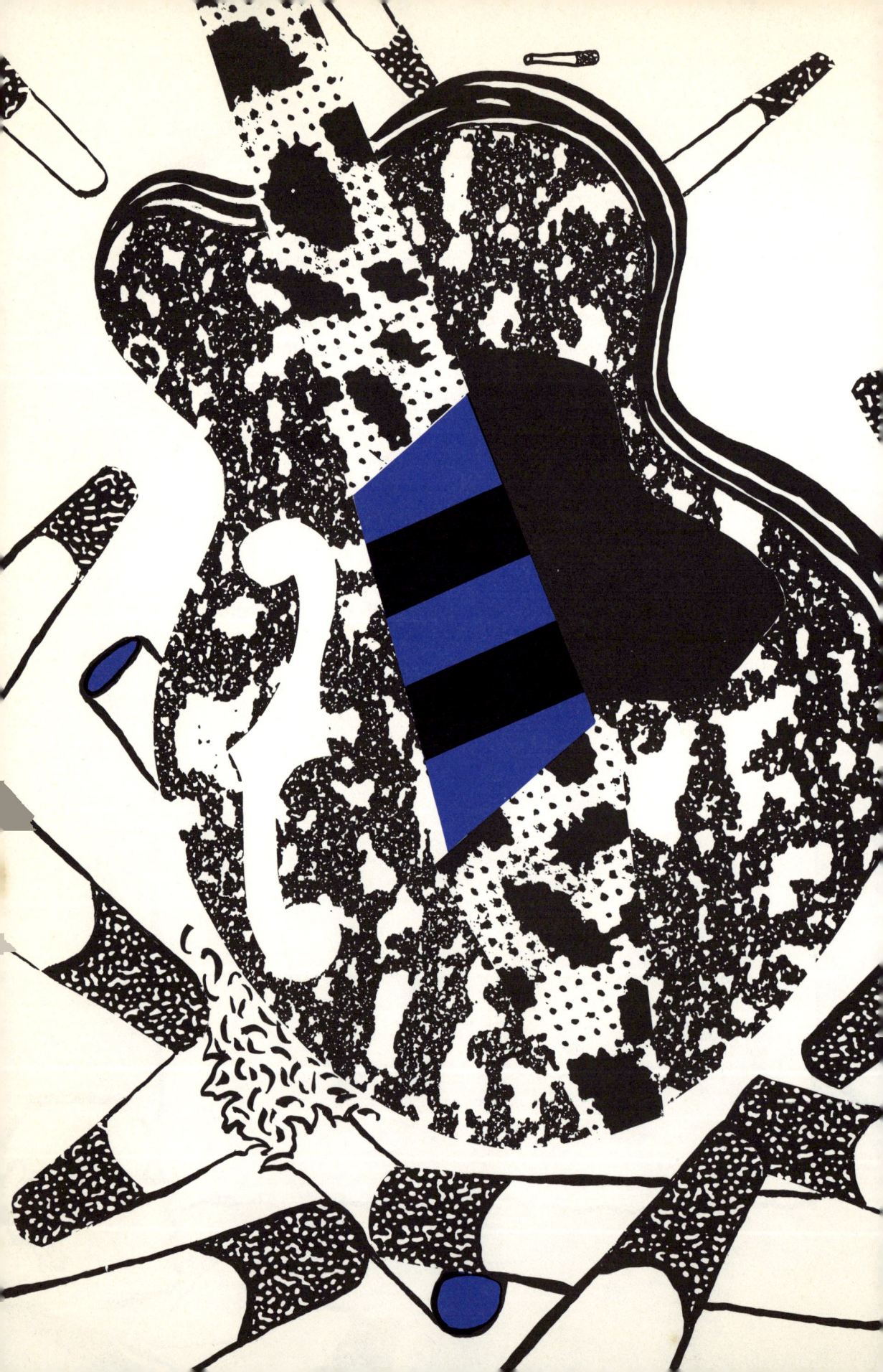

SPONSORSHIP

In late August 1986 various concerned
groups within the Australian rock music
scene defeated a proposal that would've
seen bands, venues and concerts
sponsored by a cigarette company. In
the same week, the Australian
Broadcasting Tribunal made a significant
decision that affects the amount of local
music you can hear on the radio. It
was also a week that saw corporate-
sponsored video culture move into a
domain traditionally reserved for rock 'n'
rollers. The Minister for Communications, Mr Duffy, whose responsibility it
was to assess such matters, remained
strangely quiet.

It's spring in Sydney. And it's beautiful. The off-shore winds that come from the west across the Blue Mountains to the coast have blown the city's exhaust fumes out to sea, holding up the swells for the surfers who scout the beaches looking for that wave that will shake winter off.

People are walking in the parks and the first few bright Arnotts-tin parrots are landing on the trees in the backyard. There are no clouds.

The only thing disturbing the clear blue September skies is a motorised air balloon. It's hovering over homes, cruising across the harbour, boasting a black insignia and a message for all Sydney-siders — BEER IS EXCITING: DRINK THIS BRAND NOW!

In this past week, we've had a couple of victories in the arena of the politics of dancing — the music industry.

Following two important decisions which were recently made public, Australian bands will not have to push cancer sticks to stay alive, and Australian bands will have a greater chance of getting their music played on local radio.

The first decision means that an attempt by a cigarette company to sponsor a rock circuit has been defeated. While opera, ballet, cricket, tennis, lawn bowls, jazz, rally driving, bridge — every imaginable sport and cultural activity — have all been wooed by the Faustian bargain of money for publicity, enough Australian bands have said, "No, we don't want a part of it".

The proposed Peter Jackson Rock Circuit would have meant that in return for providing promotion money for a series of venues, the company would have been allowed to associate itself with the band playing at those places: "Peter Jackson presents Throbbing Gristle", "In association with Peter Jackson, for the first time ever, The Platters" *cough, cough, splutter, splutter . . .*

130

And if the band didn't smoke, and didn't agree to playing on a stage covered with slogans and logos, or had a song about Yul Brynner in their set, then, according to a spokesman, they would not be able to play at that venue at all. The simple truth of the matter was that, denied the opportunity to advertise on TV, the cigarette company wanted to use rock bands to entice young people to take up a dangerous drug. The ''get them while they're young'' approach to market building, so successfully undertaken by banks and beer companies (to name just two experts of the art), was doomed to failure when Australian musicians showed that they were prepared to take a stand on a matter of principle. They stand alone it seems.

Of course, there were other factors involved. Some musicians had parents who'd died of lung cancer. The statistics tell it all: with an annual advertising bill in excess of $23 million, the cigarette industry contributed to a greater portion of the 20 000 tobacco and drug related deaths that took place in Oz in 1985. The ratio was about 94% tobacco to 6% for the rest.

Other musicians, no doubt, were concerned about image, an important part of being in a band. Once rock music opened itself up to promotions of this kind, would the public be able to tell who was on stage? In the racing car business, where sponsorship is the only way that the sport can be perpetuated, it's getting difficult to distinguish between the driver and the sponsor. Hence the Alan (Winfield, Johnny Walker, Kentucky Fried Chicken, Lakes Crash Repairs, Dunlop, Sony, Fosters) Jones racing team, courtesy of American Express, Westpac, BHP, Sunshine Autos . . . Enough's enough.

Then there's the spectacle of our noble sportsmen flogging grog to all and sundry.

Where there is a potential to sell then unless the vehicle for selling has a high enough regard for its own integrity — it will be used to convince others to consume.

Does Allan Border appeal to young blokes in their early teens? I suppose he does. A few people gave cricket away when the players started wearing coloured clothes and playing for a multi-national hamburger company at night; but more, it seems, are attracted by the spectacle.

Fortunately, real bands bring their own excitement with them. It comes in the form of twenty tonnes of PA and lights and a bunch of great songs. And it doesn't need to be propped up or trivialised by a barrage of cigarette advertising.

It's a great pity the government can't legislate to require the sellers of booze and cigarettes to provide a percentage of their revenue for the hospitals that are needed to look after the users. Alternatively, the revenue raised through the taxes placed on tobacco and alcohol products could be used directly for this purpose.

The other victory was the decision by the Broadcasting Tribunal (which controls the radio and TV licences) to keep the 20% Australian music requirements for all radio stations.

This quota system has meant that local music gets a reasonable amount of exposure in the face of powerful international competition. The tribunal has also introduced a bonus system for stations which play recent Australian releases and music produced by independent Australian record companies. The result is that young bands just beginning their career won't have their early records blown out the back door by the latest Michael Jackson or Bruce Springsteen release if they happen to take place on the same day.

So far so good.

But bands and performers still need somewhere to play and now two new satellite sports and entertainment stations which provide twelve hour a day programming are being introduced to club and hotel chains around Australia. These services are beamed directly to a satellite dish on location next to the beer kegs at the participating pub. But at present there is no requirement for local music to be played on these services. Consequently, the jobs of many live performers are in jeopardy.

I believe that good entertainment and great music will always find an outlet in this country. But our cultural forms need protection in this voracious age. By restricting access to the places where performers can actually perform, in order to allow for corporate image making and product selling to operate, means that a balance between the two needs to be established and regulated by the politicians whose responsibility these matters are.

We know where the businessmen stand. Alan Bond — boss of Bond Corporation, pilot of the Swan Lager airship, patron of the Gold Coast private university, and sportsman extraordinaire . . . is placing the corporate $100 million dollar profit into a satellite entertainment system called Skychannel. The other one, Club Superstation, belongs to Robert Holmes a'Court, the $600 million man.

Do we develop as artists and sportspeople under the banner of the corporate logo, trained seals smiling for the camera while another kid takes up beer and cigarettes? Or do we have a go on our own? And if we choose to resist the big bucks of sponsorship, will we be protected as individuals seeking to live out that freedom that no price can be put on? We await the answer. Minister for Communication, Mr Duffy . . . where are you?

PINE GAP

On 19 October 1987 the ten year leases
on the Joint Defence Space Research
Facility at Pine Gap comes up for
renewal. It's an American operated spy
base about which Australians know very
little. Shrouded in secrecy, it is
recognised as a potential nuclear target
because its satellite reconnaissance
facilities give the United States a first-
strike capability in the event of a nuclear
war. The Australian Anti-Bases Campaign
Coalition has been formed to
co-ordinate the efforts to close Pine
Gap and all other American military
installations on Australian soil.

When a photo-reconnaissance satellite perched a cosmic spit above planet Earth can read the number plate on a panel van winding its way through the streets of Melbourne on a winter's night or when a sound-sensing sister satellite closer than the Milky Way can record messages sent by phone and telex machine from the office of People for Peace and Environment at the back of a surfboard factory on the Sunshine Coast, then the implications of having spy-base supercommunications facilities such as those operated by America from Australian soil become clearer.

The US bases in Australia — Pine Gap, Nurrungar and North West Cape — are three of the biggest pimples on the face of adolescent Australia. Despite their description as "joint facilities" (which always goes with any mention of them), the fact is that no Australians, including our own Prime Minister, can tell you anything substantial about what goes on there.

They are *secret* bases. American built and American controlled, they exist to serve the policies of that country while we, the hosts, remain in the dark. And while they carry on behind closed doors and wire fences, the mad rush of the arms race of which they are an integral part continues unabated.

Even our politicians, who allowed the bases to be built in Australia in the first place, have remained ignorant about their true role. A typical example of their lack of knowledge of what is being perpetrated from Australian soil is former Democrats' leader Don Chipp's comment in 1985 that, "I can't find out what the truth is and I'm only a member of parliament". Other politicians have been prepared to allow the veil of secrecy surrounding the bases to remain. The recent report from the Joint Committee On Defence simply admitted that it had no information before it to enable it to make any judgements about whether claims about the function of the bases were true or not. Others have been prepared to extend a *carte blanche* guarantee of not wishing to enquire about the bases: witness Mr Hawke's recent statement that his Prime Ministership is conditional upon the bases remaining in their present state.

Nestling in the hills 19 kms west of Alice Springs, Pine Gap with its white ''golf ball' antenna protectors (radomes) is probably the best known.

Pine Gap is so close to Alice Springs that residents of that Northern Territory township describe its presence as being akin to having a funnel web spider in the bedroom . . .

Code-named Merino (no second prize for guessing who the sheep are) the base has eight radomes which house receiving and transmitting satellite dishes, a large computer room with a special signals section into which no Australians are permitted entry, various service buildings and some 500 employees. Half of the employees are, by special arrangement, Australians. We provide the cooks, the gardeners and the bottle washers. The Americans provide the orders.

A self-contained base, Pine Gap is surrounded by a 7 square kilometre buffer zone dotted with audio visual sensors and patrolled by police and security guards who operate under laws that provide for arrest under virtually any circumstances, including sketching outside the front gate. Left-hand drive cars, American history books in Alice Springs high schools and regular visits to the local supermarket complete the picture.

Although it was established in the 1960s, it wasn't until 1975 (the year Prime Minister Whitlam was removed from office) that Australians discovered that Pine Gap is run by the CIA in conjunction with two other American intelligence organisations, the National Reconnaissance Agency and the highly secretive National Security Agency. The latter's role includes devising the President's codes for the launching of nuclear weapons as well as providing blanket spying operations on everyone and everything that affects America. The world is their oyster and Pine Gap is one of their most important tools.

Pine Gap acts as a ground station which receives information from satellites that have been placed in an orbit which keeps them hovering over the same part of the world at all time. One group hang over Cape Horn, the other over Borneo, thereby allowing the Americans to monitor half of the globe, from Russia across Asia and through to the Pacific. In the case of the Rhyolite type satellites which act like giant electronic vacuum cleaners, information is picked up from agents in the field and from any electronic communications that are being monitored at the time. In the form of signals, the information is beamed down to Pine Gap, analysed, and sorted by US intelligence personnel. The juicy bits are sent back to America while the rest gets eaten by a paper shredder and then buried out in the desert. Pine Gap's function and power is so insidious that it can even listen to telephone conversations made in Australia.

A further function of the base is to collect information about Soviet and Chinese missile testing, troop movements and radar emanations so as to constantly update targeting data for the United States Nuclear Command Network.

This is critical because of the American policy of seeking to "prevail" (win) in any argument with Russia. The development of new first-strike weapons systems, along with a policy of not renouncing first use, means that Pine Gap is a key part of a military system that is specifically planning for nuclear war. All from Australian soil.

Although it is often argued that the bases are here to protect the peace, this is not logical. In the first place, the justification for planning for nuclear war is that, by doing so, such planning will prevent the weapons from ever being used and will, at the same time, exert pressure on the nuclear superpowers to take positive steps towards disarmament. The reality, which is an ever increasing arms race, is the opposite of that. Instead we're witnessing the Americans engaged in the largest peace-time build up of military forces ever seen, a refusal to stop nuclear testing despite every other nation being prepared to cease and the launch of the arms race into space. In short we're seeing a deliberate and continual increase in the tempo of the march to Armageddon.

Despite the fact that Pine Gap was planned and built long before talks about arms limitation agreements began, it is claimed that the base is important because it assists in checking these arms control agreements. It has been estimated that only a tiny fraction of Pine Gap's time (about 0.3%) is spent monitoring arms control agreements. Now that the United States has seen fit to work to overthrow the only treaty between itself and the Soviet Union, the ABM (Anti-Ballistic Missile) Treaty, and since it has also decided to ignore SALT (Strategic Arms Limitation Talks II), it is hard to see how this function actually assists verification. And Australia's so-called influence with the superpower because of the bases is certainly nowhere to be seen.

The reality is that, by accommodating places like Pine Gap, we have forfeited any claim we may assume to be taken seriously about disarmament and peace.

To take control of the bases is not only essential for the process of disarmament, but it's also a much needed step towards establishing some integrity and affirming control over what happens in our own country and what might happen in the future.

The interests of Australia and the United States are not identical. As long as the US bases remain, our claim to be a sovereign nation is as false as the doctrine which says this land was not occupied prior to European settlement, and as fractured as the logic of pretending that even more superpower gun-building can make the world a safer place.

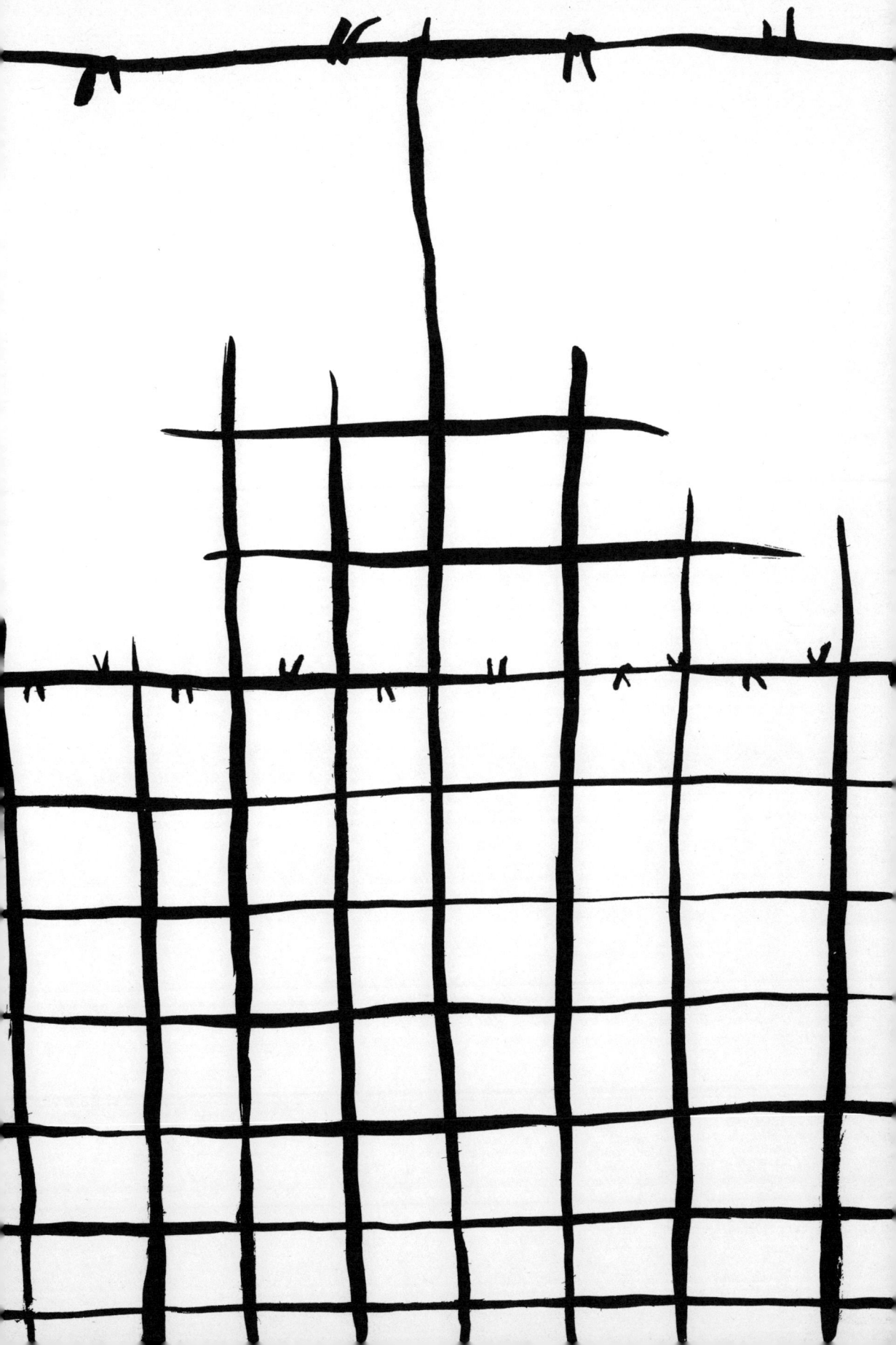